Magtymguly

Poems from Turkmenistan

Saýlanan eserler

Magtymguly
Saýlanan eserler

Giriş sözi
Türkmenistanyň Prezidenti
Gurbanguly Berdimuhamedow

Iňlis diline terjime boýunça redaktor:
Pol Maýkl Teýlor, ylymlaryň doktory
Smitson instituty

Türkmenistanyň Ylymlar akademiýasynyň habarçy-agzasy, filologiýa ylymlarynyň doktory
Annagurban Aşyrow tarapyndan türkmen dilinde çap edilen goşgular ýygyndasynyň esasynda
taýýarlanyldy
Türkmenistanyň Ylymlar akademiýasynyň Milli golýazmalar instituty

Esasy terjimeçi: **Zöhre Meredowa**
Terjime işleri boýunça utgaşdyryjy: **Maýa Meredowa**

Aziýanyň medeni taryhyny öwreniş maksatnamasy
Smitson institutynyň Türkmenistanyň Ylymlar akademiýasynyň
Milli golýazmalar instituty bilen hyzmatdaşlygynda çapa taýýarlanyldy

Magtymguly
Poems from Turkmenistan

With an Introduction by
Gurbanguly Berdimuhamedov
President of Turkmenistan

English Translation edited by
Paul Michael Taylor, Ph.D.
Smithsonian Institution

Drawn from the Turkmen edition of selected poems compiled by
Annagurban Ashirov, Ph.D.
National Institute of Manuscripts, Turkmenistan Academy of Sciences

Chief Translator: **Dr. Zohra Meredova**
Coordinator for Translations: **Maya Meredova**

Asian Cultural History Program, Smithsonian Institution
in association with the
National Institute of Manuscripts, Turkmenistan Academy of Sciences

This book is produced and distributed by: Asian Cultural History Program, Department of Anthropology, Smithsonian Institution, Washington, D.C. 20560 USA

Design by KI Graphics (Springfield, Virginia, USA). Printed in Korea.

ISBN: 978-1-891739-91-0 (hardcover)
First edition.
First printing.

Special thanks to the U.S. Department of State, Embassy of the USA in Ashgabat, Turkmenistan; Academy of Sciences of Turkmenistan; Ministry of Culture of Turkmenistan; Ministry of Foreign Affairs of Turkmenistan; and the Embassy of the Republic of Turkmenistan in Washington, D.C.

Unless otherwise noted, all photographs reproduced here are by permission of the Institute of Manuscripts, Turkmenistan Academy of Sciences, which reserves all rights to the photographs.

◄ Cover photo:
Statue of Magtymguly, erected in 2001 within the Independence Monument complex, Ashgabat, Turkmenistan.
Sculptors: Babasary Annamyradov, Nurmuhammet Atayev, Saragt Babayev, and Gylychmyrat Yarmammedov.
Bronze.

Background images:
Front & back cover: Garagum desert, Turkmenistan. Courtesy of the Ministry of Culture, Turkmenistan.
Front cover watermark image:
Manuscript of a song-poem by Magtymguly, later given the title *"Turgul" diýdiler* (*"Wake up!"- They Said*), copied in 1872-1873. Ink on paper, 20 X 16 cm.; Turkmen, written in nestaglyk font. National Institute of Manuscripts, Package 66, pp. 3-4.

► Statue of Magtymguly, with floral decorations placed for the "Days of Magtymguly Poetry" celebrations (May 2013). Statue erected in May 1971 on Magtymguly Shayoly Street in Ashgabat, Turkmenistan.
Sculptors: V.N. Vysotin and V.G. Kutumov; design by V. V. Popov.
Basalt.
Inscription on base of statue (Turkmen, in Cyrillic script) reads "Magtymguly"; Cyrillic letters have been modified to appear similar to Turkmen written in Arabic script of the kind Magtymguly would have used.

Cataloging-in-Publication Data

Magtymguly, approximately 1733-approximately 1782.
   [Poems. Selections. English]
   Magtymguly : poems from Turkmenistan / with an introduction by Gurbanguly Berdimuhamedov ; English translation edited by Paul Michael Taylor ; drawn from the Turkmen edition of selected poems compiled by Annagurban Ashyrov ; chief translator, Zohra Meredova ; coordinator for translations, Maya Meredova.
   — First edition.
     pages cm
   Added title page in Turkmen.
   ISBN-13: 978-1-891739-91-0
   1. Turkmen poetry—Translations into English. 2. Magtymguly, approximately 1733-approximately 1782—Translations into English. I. Berdimuhamedow, Gurbanguly. II. Taylor, Paul Michael, 1953- II. Ashirov, A. (Annakurban) III. Meredova, Zohra. IV. National Museum of Natural History (U.S.). Asian Cultural History Program.
   PL334.M3A2

This publication, and the Smithsonian's cooperative work with the Turkmenistan Academy of Sciences and with Turkmenistan's museums, have been made possible by generous support from Chevron.

"Magtymguly is, first and foremost,
the national poet of the Turkmen people."

From the Introduction by
Gurbanguly Berdimuhamedov
President of Turkmenistan

Introduction
Magtymguly, the Spiritual Healer of the Human Soul

Magtymguly, the great poet and thinker of the Turkmen people, has brought glory to the Turkmen people for almost three hundred years due to his name and unmatched literary heritage. Our high respect for him as a poet, and for his role in the history of the Turkmen people and its socio-political, cultural and literary life, is everlasting. Magtymguly bequeathed the Turkmen soul with the greatest faith; the Turkmen mind with the most accurate whetstone to differentiate good and evil in life; and the eyes of Turkmen with unquenchable radiance.

Magtymguly's poetical-philosophical literary heritage found its rightful place in the center of Turkmen people's heart as a song of the greatest love for the Almighty, Motherland, human beings, nature and human life. It would be underestimated if one tried to judge Magtymguly only as a poet and evaluate his literary heritage only through the lens of the creative style and poetic value. Magtymguly is the kind of poet, the kind of philosopher, who could contribute not only to the development of the Turkmen, but to the whole world's philosophical thought, who brought radiance to universal creative mind, and who was able to provide a masterful artistic depiction of secular life. Magtymguly finely paved his way to people's souls and found an eternal place in their hearts thanks to his masterful application of a variety of the best and most exquisite methods of presenting thoughts, uniting his philosophic thoughts about the world, humanity, Motherland and love with delicate human feelings.

Magtymguly is, first and foremost, the national poet of the Turkmen people. While he looks at all human beings with love, this great thinker's love and tenderness toward his own people are incomparable in their magnitude. It is his boundless love for his people, for his Motherland, and it is his ideas full of the spirit of battle for the fate of his people, that took him beyond the national boundaries and turned him into the universal poet of mankind. It is truly so since the one who keeps his dignity high, respects and lifts the dignity of all people to new heights. The one who loves his own people is able to love all other people. The poet's influential and deep philosophical views about the perfection of the world, about human being and about life during his epoch when he preached among people, as well as his edifications about the perfection of the human soul and of society — these were the fruits of his endless love for his people.

Magtymguly called his contemporaries and all people to strive to understand the true sources of a happy life, of a fair society, and the deep and full meaning of everything that took place in their lives, during their epoch. He urged all people to acknowledge wisdom, to understand their inner selves and to learn what national identity means. The great poet, who dreamed about peace and prosperity, and about the development of science, education and culture in his native land, left us an immense legacy of beautiful poetic treasure filled with wisdom and delicate feelings. The fine and perfected thoughts of his exquisite verses served as a worthy guideline not only for the future of the Turkmen nation, but for the everyday life and spiritual needs of all humanity. This is exactly why the significance of his poetic world went beyond national boundaries and turned into a repository of the human wisdom, a cultural treasure of world literature. The creative works of Magtymguly give spiritual joy not only to the Turkmen people, but to all mankind. Moreover, the poet's creative work makes people think about social aspects of life as well. It is for this reason his beautiful verses that are sung in songs, and that became an indispensable part of the human wisdom were translated and are being translated into many languages.

Magtymguly is a spiritual healer of the human soul. Admonition and advice, expressed by the poet in his verses, serve as a healing balm for the human spirit; as wings for the aspiring soul; as an engine for new achievements. It is for this reason that despite the passage of many epochs, and despite the transformations of life styles, the value of the poetry is not lost but rather becomes more and more significant. His verses provide relief to the wounded heart, strength to the tired body and wings of aspiration to the gloomy spirit. Due to these characteristics Turkmen people always turned to the poet as a healer for their pains and sufferings during their times of hardships, trouble, hesitation and grief. Magtymguly's healing verses were able to purify the soul of young and old during any period of history; to inspire love for this beautiful world, humanity and life; to lift people's spirits high, and to ensure the spiritual health of Turkmen society. It is very true that his poetry provided relief to the human soul like fresh and pure water, flowing right from a mountain spring. His verses are pure and fresh like the morning breeze. They please our soul like the fragrance of the wild flowers and sweet basil, roses and poppy flowers, abounding in the meadows. They excite and inspire us like a tender and sweet melody of the dutar[1] relieving us from stress and worries, penetrating our inner soul and body. Therefore, Magtymguly's poetry is indeed a healing spiritual balm that consolidates all healing components necessary for the health of the human being.

Magtymguly lived in a very complicated and difficult historical period. Magtymguly is a great figure that perfected himself by going through many strong upheavals, by overcoming many personal and social sufferings, and by being part of the spiritual climate of that period. The poet reached the highest level of perfection and became an impeccable individual who was fully aware of the world surrounding him, who could distinguish good and evil in the society, life and people, who deeply mastered all of the religious and secular sciences discovered by his time, and who had passed all the stages of spiritual perfection. Magtymguly, the great thinker, among his thoughts universally beneficial for the entirety humankind, specifically urged the Turkmen people, who were unintegrated and dispersed in various corners of the world at the time, for statehood, unity and national consolidation. The greatness of Magtymguly lies in the fact that he was the first person to consider all Turkmen, who were spread out and unintegrated at that time, as one nation and to preach widely the ideas of unity and statehood.

The poet's childhood took place at the time when Turkmen people were ruled by the *Owshar* Turkmen tribe, but his adulthood coincided with the rule of the *Gajar* Turkmen tribe. It is true that both of the ruling clans were Turkmen. But neither of these ruling elites was willing to give enough attention to the national aspirations and benefits of the Turkmen people, thus creating dissatisfaction in the hearts of Turkmen people and Magtymguly. One could hardly call any of these states as a national Turkmen state of the kind that was longed for by the people and by the poet himself. Therefore, Magtymguly wrote these verses at that time: "There are too many sufferings in this motherland, in this time I live in," openly revealing his perception of the world at that time. During these complicated and harsh times Magtymguly was searching for the way to "better the fate of the people" and "to bring the eternal spring to his native land". Wherever he travelled, "wandering among people," — be it Bukhara, Khiva, Afghanistan, India or Turkey — his

---

[1] Traditional two-stringed Turkmen lute, used to accompany the singing of poems like these. (—Ed.)

thoughts, dreams, and worries were always about the fate of the Turkmen land, about the Turkmen people and their fate.

In the eighteenth century there was a significant obstacle for realization of the fundamental social idea of Magtymguly "to unite all Turkmen tribes." During that century there was a strong discord among many different Turkmen tribes, and each tribe had to search for its own way of survival. In the absence of the unified national state, each tribe's search for protection had fostered discord and alienation from the other. Moreover, there were a number of active shadow forces which worked under their own agenda to escalate animosity among tribes. In those circumstances, the sage Magtymguly was consistently reiterating his conception that the biggest enemy of his people was their own fragmentation and the discord among the tribes; that it was necessary to establish mutual understanding between tribes, and that all tribes should unite to serve one purpose and one state. He strived to fill his people's minds with the idea that they had to struggle for the establishment of the whole Turkmen nation, for a strong and stable Turkmen state, and that was the only way "for the Turkmen fate to prosper," to wipe away any evil invaders from intruding into the nation and the state:

> When souls, hearts and minds of tribes are united,
> Their troops when gathered will melt stones and ground on their way,
> When Turkmen gather around one table to share a meal,
> The destiny of Turkmen will rise high.

This idea of Magtymguly is understood by all and appeals to the hearts of everyone. This poem has served the Turkmen people as a national anthem during the eighteenth and nineteenth centuries. But how could this brilliant idea be accomplished, how could "all unintegrated tribes be gathered around one table?" The great thinker put forward an initiative of consolidating around one personality, and "listening to one person" to achieve that goal. It should be noted that despite all the hardships and challenges of his time, the poet never lost his hope for the prosperous and happy future for his nation.

Magtymguly's greatest contribution for his Turkmen people is his constant fight for unity, and his hatred for fragmentation and discord among the Turkmen tribes. One can see that for a long time many generations of Turkmen people were learning, and they are still learning, the lessons of the great thinker Magtymguly about national unity. Time has proven true Magtymguly's brilliant idea of the sovereign state.

Today, the dreams of Magtymguly about a happy and prosperous future for his nation have been realized. Independent and neutral Turkmenistan has honorably taken its place on the world map as the land of peace and unity. Turkmen people, who strongly believe in the miracle of unity, will always be grateful to Magtymguly. For the great poet's brilliant ideas, wise admonitions and lessons about unity will always be vital for the further stability and prosperity of our state. Respect for Magtymguly rises higher and higher during this epoch of happiness in our sovereign state. The great thinker's thoughts and multifaceted ideas deeply connected to life and social issues, which became an integral part of the universal treasury of the whole of mankind, serve as a spiritual foundation of our developed society.

Gurbanguly Berdimuhamedov
President of Turkmenistan

Preface to the English Translation of Magtymguly's Poems

The poems presented in English translation here have been selected to illustrate the range of topics encompassed and the types of poetry produced by the great eighteenth century poet of the Turkmen people, Magtymguly Pyragy. These poems have been selected from the 393 Turkmen-language poems compiled by Dr. Annagurban Ashirov of Turkmenistan's Institute of Manuscripts, and published in 2013.[1] That two-volume compilation was itself a sampling of over 700 surviving poems thought to have been composed by Magtymguly. These poems were traditionally sung by Turkmen singers known as *bagshy*, who as they sang played the two-stringed Turkmen instrument called *dutar*. While many of Magtymguly's poems are known from early manuscripts (though currently no manuscripts from the poet's own hand have been located), many others survived only in these traditionally sung formats, up until recent efforts to record the songs and transcribe the poems (lyrics) in written form.

The Smithsonian's involvement in presenting this English translation of selected poems by Magtymguly grew out of our on-going cultural exchanges since 2011 with the museums and cultural institutions of Turkmenistan, carried out with the much appreciated support and assistance of the U.S. Department of State, and with generous support from Chevron. These exchanges have included two exhibitions of Turkmen art in Washington, D.C. (in 2011 and 2013) and their associated publications[2], and many seminars and workshops on museum and preservation issues in Turkmenistan. The works of Magtymguly, considered Turkmenistan's "national poet," have exerted a profound influence on the performing and visual arts of that country. Yet many non-Turkmen have been at a disadvantage in seeing this due to the paucity of English translations available. Magtymguly's poems are sung at festive occasions, and favorite lines cited frequently by people of all walks of life. In recent years, within Turkmenistan's craft and visual art traditions, we also see the image of Magtymguly invoked as regional elements are brought together into artworks expressing the national narrative of a unified Turkmenistan, corresponding to the "dream" expressed in the poetry of this eighteenth century poet. For this reason we have given this selection of his poems the English title *Magtymguly: Poems from Turkmenistan*. Admittedly one could argue that Turkmenistan did not exist yet in the eighteenth century, but it existed as a longed-for unified place in the poet's imagination; and in any case the poems come from and deeply express perspectives that are a common source of inspiration within Turkmenistan today.

---

1 *Magtymguly: Eserler ýygyndysy,* compiled by A. Ashirov [Turkmen: A. Aşyrow]; edited by R. Godarov [Turkmen: R. Godarow]. Ashgabat: Institute of Manuscripts, Turkmenistan Academy of Sciences [Türkmenistanyň Ylymlar akademiýasynyň, Milli golýazmalar instituty], 2013.

2 *Turkmenistan: Ancient Arts Today,* by Paul Michael Taylor, Trevor Loomis Merrion, Jasper Waugh-Quasebarth, and William Bradford Smith. Washington, D.C.: Asian Cultural History Program, Smithsonian Institution, 2011. *Turkmenistan: Arts from the Land of Magtymguly,* by Paul Michael Taylor, Trevor Loomis Merrion, William Bradford Smith, and Jasper Waugh-Quasebarth. Washington, D.C.: Asian Cultural History Program, Smithsonian Institution, 2013.

Another testament to Magtymguly's importance within Turkmenistan today, as national poet and national hero, is that the President of Turkmenistan, Gurbanguly Berdimuhamedov, has provided an introductory essay to use in this volume. We include our translation of his Introduction here, at the request and with the permission of our counterpart organization for this project, the Turkmenistan Academy of Sciences (Institute of Manuscripts). It is an unmatched and authentic indication, now available to readers of English, of the significance of Magtymguly in Turkmenistan's present-day philosophical and cultural life.

With respect to the translation and format of the poems presented here, it must be added that none of these poems originally had a "title," Poem titles shown here in English are translations of their now-accepted or "standard" Turkmen titles first systematically given in a 1926 edition of Magtymguly's poems compiled by Berdy Kerbabayev based on an earlier manuscript in Arabic script. I have included at the end of this book a table of equivalents so that readers wishing to find the original Turkmen text for any poem can locate that within the 2013 volumes compiled by Dr. Ashirov, using these titles.

This book's publication coincides with Turkmenistan's celebration, in 2014, of the 290th anniversary of Magtymguly's birth (1724), a fact which may surprise international scholars accustomed to seeing his birth and death dates routinely listed (as they are in

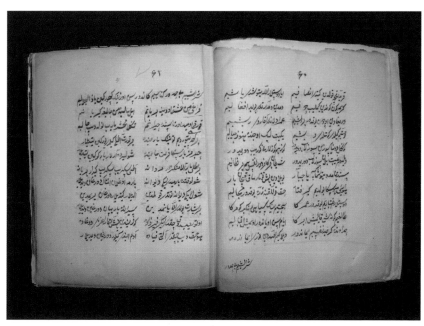

Manuscript of a poem by Magtymguly, later given the title *Yetişdi salym* ("I Reached that Age"), copied early twentieth century. Ink on paper, 22 X 18 cm.; Turkmen, written in nestaglyk font. National Institute of Manuscripts, Package 610, pp. 60-61. (English translation below, p. 62).

This manuscript shows some of the careful paper conservation work being carried out within Turkmenistan's Institute of Manuscripts. Comparable research and preservation efforts on poems preserved as songs, within a performance tradition, are being carried out at Turkmenistan's National Conservatory. The Smithsonian's Asian Cultural History Program, in conjunction with the Embassy of the U.S.A. in Turkmenistan, is working with museums and cultural repositories of Turkmenistan on these preservation and research efforts.

Library of Congress bibliographic records) as "approximately 1733 to approximately 1782," meaning the poet would have died around age 49. Those commonly cited birth and death dates have long been based on the accounts of Turkmen visited by Arminius Vámbéry in 1863,[3] without further confirmation. Turkmen readers have long questioned the accuracy of those dates, however, as readers of these translations might do also considering Magtymguly's descriptions of what seem to be his own experiences at an advanced age in some of the poems. While recognizing that any such dates are estimates in the absence of independent evidence, the detailed study of Magtymguly's poetry, including calendrical references and autobiographical details given in conjunction with known historical facts, leads Ashirov in his recent re-evaluation[4] to argue forcefully that Magtymguly's likely year of birth was 1724, and likely year of death as late as 1807, a considerably different timespan. In any case this eighteenth century poet has deeply affected Turkmen life continuously up to the present day.

I wish to express my thanks and admiration to Dr. Annagurban Ashirov and all his staff at the Institute of Manuscripts, Turkmenistan Academy of Sciences, for their continuing manuscript preservation and philological work on Magtumguly's texts. Special thanks also to the primary translator of this volume, Dr. Zohra Meredova. For their assistance with this translation project, sincere thanks are also due to the staff of the U.S. Embassy in Ashgabat, especially translation coordinator Maya Meredova, Cultural Affairs Officer Michael Cavey, and Public Affairs Officer Brian Stimmler; and to those at the Smithsonian who assisted with the editorial work: Trevor L. Merrion, William Bradford Smith and Adam Simons. We especially thank Chevron for its generous support for this translation and for the collaborative work with museums and scholarly institutions of Turkmenistan which preceded it. Within Chevron, we thank Dr. Diana Sedney of Chevron's Washington office and Mr. Hector Fajardo, President of Chevron Nebitgaz B.V. Turkmenistan, and their staffs. We gratefully acknowledge the help of the Ministry of Culture and Ministry of Foreign Affairs of Turkmenistan, and the Embassy of Turkmenistan in Washington, D.C., USA.

Paul Michael Taylor
Director, Asian Cultural History Program
Smithsonian Institution

---

3 Vámbéry, Arminius. *Travels in Central Asia, being the account of a journal from Teheran across the Turkoman desert on the eastern shore of the Caspian to Khiva, Bokhara, and Samarcand performed in the year 1863.* London: John Murray, 1864.

4 Ashirov, Annagurban. "Magtymguly Pyragy" Pp. 377-399 in: *Magtymguly. Eserler ýygyndysy.* (vol. 1), ibid., 2013.

Poems

The Land of the Turkmen

Between the Jeyhun[1] river and the Hazar[2] sea,
The wind of the Turkmen land rises above its deserts,
Its blossoming flowers are as precious as the apples of my black eyes,
Torrents rush from the slopes of its tall black mountains.

The Almighty blessed this land with His care,
The herds of thoroughbred camels graze in its deserts,
Its green meadows will blossom with colorful flowers,
The Turkmen steppes are filled with sweet basil.

Its fairies will appear in their colorful dresses,
The sweet smell of ambergris will fill the air all around,
The beg, töre and elderly are owners of the country,
The beautiful land of the Turkmen will be filled with populated and prosperous villages.

He is a son of a brave man, his forefathers were brave,
Görogly is his brother, his enthusiasm is high,
If hunters hunt for him in the mountains or steppes,
A Turkmen, the son of a lion, won't be caught alive.

When souls, hearts and minds of tribes are united,
Their troops when gathered will melt stones and ground on their way,
When Turkmen gather around one table to share a meal,
The destiny of Turkmen will rise high.

The spirits get high when on a horseback,
Its mountains, at a glance, look like rubies,
When its rivers are full-flowing, bringing honey within,
No dam can withstand the floods of the Turkmen land.

They will not be taken unaware by intruders, nor trampled down in battle;
They are not dependent on either a curse or violence,
They will neither wither nor yearn when separated from a nightingale,
The flowers of the Turkmen will always spread the fragrance of the ambergris.

All tribes are in brotherhood, all clans are at peace,
Their destinies won't go counter; they are the Creator's blessing,
If the brave straddle their horses, the battle will be over,
The only path Turkmen take is toward the intruders.

They will have their spirits high and be cool inside,
They will crumble stones; nothing can stop them on their way,
I won't cast a glance anywhere else; my soul will not take joy,
Magtymguly, the elderly of Turkmen will have his say.

The Foundation of the Turkmen

You should know - whatever I am building, is, in fact, the core of the earth
It will always be free, this is the foundation of the Turkmen.

Enemies confronting them lose all their hopes,
You should know – out of steel is made this Turkmen fortress.

King Solomon, brave Rüstem u Zal, King Jemshit - all wanted to conquer it,
No Shah's evil will damage it even when an army of a hundred thousand soldiers assault daily.

Mountains will learn from it, its armies stand in rows,
Each time when Zulpukar is raised, a young man's enthusiasm increases.

If Teke, Yomut, Yazyr, Goklen, and residents of Ahal are together united,
Flowers will start to blossom when they march together.

If all Kizilbash are thrown behind mountains,
They won't sleep at night or dawn – their weeping will be continousy heard.

If a hunter steps forward, he won't succeed
He won't be able to lure Turkmen children into his hostage.

The wise are numerous in the Turkmen land, as are events worth celebrating.
Its brave people are men of their word, and their hearts are open.

Magtymguly keeps saying: there is no evil in their hearts.
For the Almighty takes care of this land with His blessings.

"Wake Up!" - They Said

Once in mid night when I was sleeping,
Four horsemen came, "Wake up!" they said,
"We have a message to you at this moment,
We'd like you to go, see those brave men."

At seeing those four brave men,
My heart's beat sped up, my head got dizzy,
The two men standing by my side ordered:
"Don't stand here, my son, go over there."

Those two men held me by my arms,
Taking me away from where I stood,
There came a signal then to me,
"Keep quiet and stand steady!" they said.

We hardly sat, and then two white-headed elderly men arrived,
With tears running down their cheeks, with prayers whispered from their lips,
Six men more came on foot, shouting,
"Here they are! Now, look at the people coming!" - They said.

Four more horsemen came, all dressed in green,
With green canes, and stallions black,
"The room for the council is too small,
For the people are many – set it wider then," they said.

They saw sixty other riders approaching from afar,
All greeted a man, saying "Mohammad!"
Each inquiring about his health,
"Do not stay here, let's go to the large room!" they said.

We were put behind a rider on a saddle,
Quietly they entered the room, stood waiting,
Finally all gathered and the council started,
"Young man," they said, "Come join us."

"This is Ali" – they said, he shook my hand,
He took a palliasse from under me,
And poured I knew not what upon my head:
"Live the life you're destined for!" they said.

I asked Haidar to introduce all of them to me one by one,
"That one is our dear Prophet, don't shun him,
That's Eslim Hoja, there's Baba Zuryat,
Here's Veys–al–Karani, do not forget!" - They said.

"That's Bahauddin, also a famous one,
Here is Zengi Baba, famed beyond comparison,
And next, leaning on each other are the Four Companions,
"So, speak up, let your intention be known to us," they said.

Suddenly some young and elderly also present there said,
"Why not give a blessing to this young man –
This is all you have to know," they said,
"These are one hundred twenty four thousand prophets and companions,"

Now the Prophet said, "Oh, Shahymerdan,
Oh, Eslim Hoja, Oh, Selman Baba,
Abu Bakr Siddiq, or Omar, Osman
Grant the wish of this young man," he said.

Eslim and Baba Salman ordered a brave man,
They poured a cup of liquid, which made me suffer,
I lay down there swooning and with no motion,
"See what's there on earth and Heaven" – they said.

I turned into wind and reached earth's core,
My view reached the Heaven's belt,
"The secrets of the Almighty in the universe of angels –
All have to be seen by you"- They said.

Whatever I wished I could reach,
Wherever I looked I could view,
Lying down peacefully in the state I was in,
With saliva on my face, "Wake up!" they said.

The Prophet said "Come on, companions,
Give him your blessings and see this young man off,"
And he ordered the four horsemen,
"Take him back to where he has come from!" –he said.

Thus Magtymguly woke up, opened his eyes,
He wondered what thoughts had gone through his mind,
With white foam around his mouth resembling a baby camel just breastfed,
"Go, young man, may God be your companion," they said.

Known to the World

Oh, my friends, my dear friends, my beloved, who is dearer to me than my life,
Is known to all in this world, which is as dear as a soul.

I'll certainly go to her regardless what fords must be crossed,
I will surely settle my home only there where she belongs.

The beloved would say: I will kill my beloved with my own hands,
But for that to happen, depression should severely capture me first.

If others when in love are enslaved with the beauty of their beloved's hair,
Poor me, my love for her has tied up both my legs and hands.

When your beloved is full of joy, having a feast with others,
Find courage within yourself to say openly: "That poor man is in grief."

The spring will come, time will pass, and my eyes will sink in gloom,
They won't obey me thus won't open; they are in such a deep sleep.

When asked by those who don't know, tell them my poor name,
That I am Gerkez, my motherland is Etrek and my name is Magtymguly.

Goklen

When in the desert, Goklen[3]
Will act like a deer or kulan,[4]
When inspired going into battle,
Goklen will turn into a hungry lion.

He won't abandon the land of his people,
Neither trouble nor disaster will impact him,
Oh, Goklen, I hope you prove my words—
If God is willing.

Mowlam has inspired me,
Thanks to you we are blessed,
No one will encroach upon you,
Come back to Gurgen, Goklen.

God prompts my words,
It is enough to utter them once,
Those who come with evil,
Will ask you for mercy, Goklen.

If a servant becomes effusive,
Nishapur will issue a decree,
And this era will become the epoch,
For all of the Muslims, Goklen.

Khorasan will turn into ruins,
Leveled by horses,
They won't march as far as Mazenderan,
And come to a decision, Goklen.

Your faith will remain as the light of God,
Your strength will increase as the power of Rome,
You'll fight like a hungry jackal,
Marching in the field, Goklen!

Your troops will be strong in the battle,
Your statehood will become more robust,
In the fight with Kizilbash,
You will be able to conquer Iran, Goklen!

Addressing the Great God,
I wish that your wealth may increase,
Pyragy says, leading your troops
You will reach Tehran, Goklen!

No One Knows Where It Begins or Ends

To defend its honor, the tribes of Goklen and Yomut
Gathered such an army, that no one knows where it begins or ends,
The desert Deshti-Dahan had not space enough to hold it,
One won't know its paths or the lands it stopped.

If crows attack it, its falcons will fight back,
Mountains and rocks tremble at its threat,
Even the dead will wake up and fight against those who are alive,
One won't know its lions, foxes or wolves.

Three thousand of its soldiers carried spears,
Four thousand of its elephant riders are capable of crushing the castle,
If Salyr and Teke tribes will join from the top,
One won't know the enemy's courage or cowardice.

All Sunnis will gather together to defend their dignity,
They will demolish fortresses, and destroy gardens,
Their giant-like forces will conquer the city of Isfahan,
No one knows whether the number of the conquered cities will be three or four.

Magtymguly, this battlefield is the field of Ali,
Look, what will be the deeds of Omar, Osman,
The earth and sky is full of the horses' breath,
No one would know where the Khorasan's soil used to be.

We Shed Our Tears

My fortune seems to be taking wing,
We prayed and shed our tears,
Praying for the fulfillment of our wishes, oh, Great Lord,
Unexpectedly the Kizilbash have betrayed us and left.

May people prosper and spread around all over the steppes of the land seen by Hydyr,
Let the foundation of our homeland get stronger and last forever,
May our wild and joyful youth come to their senses,
And all enjoy food cooked and served on one table.

Let the souls of dervishes join together in a prayer,
And the young gather for conversation and music,
May never-ending spring fall on to my people,
May winter last not more than ninety days as scheduled.

If only Turkmen become united and serve one common goal,
They could dry out the Red Sea, as well as the river Nile,
So let the tribes of Teke, Yomut, Goklen, Yazir, and Alili,
All five unite and serve one ruler as one nation.

Magtymguly, understands not to leave any Muslim
To the torture of the infidel while a soul is alive,
Give a blessing for the union of Yomut and Goklen,
And let Kemal Khan Afghani be our leader.

For Chovdur Khan

People hoped to ask for the help of,
Ahmet Shah for Chovdur Khan,
It was a destiny to go and not to come,
Back safe and sound for Chovdur Khan.

Trees have curdled, rains have stopped,
Clouds have slowed down, unable to tolerate this pain,
The earth has degraded and destinies gotten furious,
Even deserts turned into a paradise for Chovdur Khan.

The death has become outrageous, eager to break the balance wheel,
The fate wished to grant him with tenderness,
The river has overflown to kill his thirst,
The lakes submerged for Chovdur Khan.

Your people stayed behind with hope in their hearts,
Your beloved Annahal was waiting with hope deep inside,
Your brother Atanazar had nothing to do but grieve over you,
Covering long distances in search for Chovdur Khan.

Sultans and khans know his value when he comes,
People were left in ambiguity – his repentance is in his soul,
The death or the fate brought you to Yezd, Kerman;
Maybe blood kin attracted you, Chovdur Khan.

Oracles became deaf and dumb, whereas fortune-tellers told only bitter predictions;
The rains became a barrier, roads dangerous,
The springs dried out, the stones turned into wax,
The tongues became eloquent for Chovdur Khan.

Speak out Magtymguly, let the world know,
Let them become witnesses that he is in paradise;
Let people pray, saying "May the Lord be merciful,"
And the entire nation joins in this prayer for Chovdur Khan.

Chovdur Khan

Goklen and Yomut are out on the road looking around,
With the hope that Chovdur Khan will come safe and sound,
Mullahs and mufti join in the prayer to the Lord,
And have finished their reading of the Koran, Chovdur Khan.

Birds flew over the mountains in their search,
Fish emptied all the waters in search of the road,
Girls and women have cut their silk red coats,
Cotton dresses and robes, Chovdur Khan.

The mountains have bent their heads, got covered with mist,
The winds became too weak to rise up and blow,
The Moon and Sun have both set, Mars has risen,
The clouds started pouring, Chovdur Khan.

Shepherds returned, leaving their herds behind,
Fishes abandoned their waters and came out to the banks,
People not being able to tolerate all this,
All started to moan, Chovdur Khan.

Merchants forgot their distant trading routes,
Traders have returned back their goods,
The Moon and Sun have both set; the dawn has broken with a sigh,
All living creatures are repenting, Chovdur Khan.

Those who travelled to India came back,
Inquiring of your brave name, joined in whimpering,
Oracles predicting from the sacred book,
Were unable to find a remedy for your pain, Chovdur Khan.

A hunter's stretched arrow stayed in the bow,
Your name shook the whole universe, Chovdur Khan,
There is no end to the moaning heard,
Even Turan will go down weeping for you, Chovdur Khan.

Magtymguly, my courageous falcon has flown away,
My protector, my solicitor, my brother,
My gray-haired head is unable to make sense of this,
The heavy mist encompassed it, Chovdur Khan.

You Are Mourned

Chovdur Khan, the iris of my eyes, the pillar of my soul,
You died, you are mourned,
The fighter for the Goklen, wanted by the people,
You left your people unprotected, Chovdur Khan.

The foes wouldn't dare to come when you were here,
The ones who came regretted much seeing your strength and power,
They couldn't reach the land of the Goklens, over the mountains,
You left us among snakes.

The fate had made your blossoming life fade,
Severe wind had torn away your buds,
Mountains raised their heads in sympathy,
Filling their eyes with tears in mist and snow.

Who is that lucky one to get the bow of Isfahan?
Take my word for granted, your place is in paradise;
Goklen and Yomut – your palaces are ruined,
Fate has destroyed them as something not needed.

Magtymguly, your entrusted friend, your wise adviser,
He is unable to hold back his tears,
Mist has covered the mountains' belts and tops,
Days and months have passed in endless mourning.

Dovletali

It becomes a pillar for Sunnis, a barrier for infidels,
If Dovletali sharpens his sword,
It becomes a destan[5] for the universe,
A message for his people if Dovletali speaks up.

His words became a behest for his people,
A shelter for the poor in wretched days,
In the far lands, in the neighborhoods,
Friends and enemies are pleased with Dovletali.

During all his life he conquered a lot,
Until the Creator put an end to his life;
Living a happy life in this world until he died,
The spring of Dovletali had never ended.

Misfortune will touch anyone it chooses,
One won't avoid his fate if it is decided;
An eagle would be defeated if a falcon so wished,
A lion would be tricked by the skill of Dovletali.

He has a large tribe and a great nation,
When united they are famous and known to the world,
With a sword in the battlefield, eloquent in
The Council of State, Dovletali is equal to one hundred.

If he wishes, the frozen stones will melt,
If he is angry, mountains will follow his orders,
Brighter than the Sun and purer than the Moon,
The star of Dovletali is high in the sky.

He is the commander, sultan to countless people,
He is merciless as a lion in the battlefield,
His abode is a Mosque, his home is the Council,
Throughout days and nights for Dovletali.

His entreaty goes as far as the heavens,
He is a leopard in the forest, a tiger in the mountains,
He is an anchor on a ship, a raft in a river,
Wherever Dovletali goes.

The wretched will cry over you,
No one was able to help you,
His horse was left behind in the gardens, his companion is left on the road.
The message of Dovletali will never be known.

Magtymguly, he left this world having no one equal to him,
Having no match for his position or courage,
Having no sons like the prophet, and no end like Solomon,
The end of Dovletali will be just like that.

"He Left this World," They Said

Oh, dear friends, a nasty destan came to its end,
"A hero left this world," they said,
The end of the world has come, the Sun darkened,
"The Sun and the Moon have set," they said.

An expected pain of separation came,
Seidi Tarhan will suffer the pain of separation,
The harvest of his life – the lonely candle,
"Was blown off by a great storm," they said.

Ovezgeldi has gone, as well as other things,
A discourse has ended, happiness turned into sadness,
Brothers, trusted friends, close ones and strangers,
"All wore black and cried," they said.

He who had a divine horse, a sturdy belt, as well as full ammunition,
Devoted to his state, splendor and wealth,
He who had many guests, wealth and a palace,
"His great horde is now abandoned," they said.

The suffering from solitude will pass,
It is the worst of all to be left with no sons,
One's place will be lost without the heir,
"His caravan has moved leaving nothing behind," they said.

Magtymguly, the great man of Turkestan,
A brave one, the trusted servant of Soyunhan,
The glory of the army, the core of the battle,
"The earth has taken him now," they said.

You Are the Sultan, Abdullah

Mazenderan is your land, your country,
You are the sultan of this land, Abdullah,
God, I was lucky for the chance to see him,
You are the basil of those gardens, Abdullah.

Both Baghdad and Turan need your service,
So does Arkach in the north, and Iran in the south,
You are well known in Rome and Europe,
You are the treasure and diamond of Bulgaria, Abdullah.

The Shah of Bulgaria sent you a message,
The Almighty granted you His mercy,
You are blessed by the Prophet's ummah,
You are the spirit of the spring of life, Abdullah.

Arabia and India are in great need of you,
Turkestan shakes at your high-pitched voice,
Mountainous Georgia sent you many gifts,
You are the supporter of Afghani masters, Abdullah.

You resemble Rustem, the son of Zal,
You are engaged to a fine girl like Hatyja,
Sixty men are in your service,
You are the hero of the world, Abdullah.

The Shah of Turkestan trembles at your order,
All, poor and rich, are in need of you,
Your one word embraces a thousand prayers,
I shall write this destan, Abdullah.

Pyragy is just God's sinful servant,
No one knows their destiny,
If you wished for beautiful fairies of paradise, they would be around you,
The khan of all young men, Abdullah.

The Eminence Is Yours

The son of the leader Fath, the time has come for you to govern,
This time of happiness is yours again,
The old state will bring you new happiness,
Your path is the path of eminence, of leadership.

All, blessed by Ilyas, in the waters wrapped in clouds,
All, blessed by Kowus, in the mountains wrapped in mist,
The city in the desert blessed by Hydyr,
All the riches created by the Almighty are yours.

You will bury with gifts your close ones and strangers,
Your fate will ruin all who come with ill intentions,
Your treasury — diamonds of Jahangir,
Badahshan mines and rubies – all are yours.

He, who confronts your anger will turn to dust,
He, who confronts your mercy will reach the heavens,
The throne of eminence suits you,
Feridun's unique fate is yours.

The bows built on the thrones of Samarkand,
Like Mahti you withstand the devastation,
Like Suleyman, you can make the water obey,
Like Alexander the Great, the river crossing is yours.

If you march toward the east, you'll reach Khorosan,
First you will conquer the Kurds, then Yazyr Khan,
Iraq and Isfahan will be also conquered by you,
All the cavalry of Dagestan is yours.

My words will not be wasted, they will become true,
My look is alchemic; it can turn copper into gold.
The state invaded by the Persian will become yours,
Now all dreams of this world are yours.

The young men will be protecting you
Hydyr, Ilyas will lead your horse in the race,
Eleven imams will provide you their support,
Imam Ali will rein your horse.

Magtymguly says, it won't wake on its own like Rome,
It is strong like Alexander the Great; it won't be defeated, won't be crushed,
Like mountains it won't shake, like a river it won't go back,
This land, the land of Yomut and Goklen, is yours.

To the Top of the Heavens

Oh, Ahmet Shah, your fame spreads all over the earth,
Your name will reach the top of the heavens,
Whoever comes is on your side, those who don't become your game
Climb the stairs of greatness, step by step.

Invade Iran, lead the army,
Let your crown sit strong on your head,
You are the king of the lions in the Humayun Mountains,
You are like a giant fish in a raging river.

You are the lion, longing for a hunt in the forests,
You are the brain of the Byzantine Empire, one of the giants,
You are the one who can withstand the arrow of the son of Zal,
You are known to the misfortunate like the son of Gushtasp.

If your aim is Iran, your origin is Turan,
Your friends are pleased with your work, and your enemies are surprised,
Your fate will grant you luck, success will be with you,
If you concentrate your merciful look in one place.

Pyragy says, you will bring success to the religion,
You are the King of Kings, a pillar of Islam,
Make the land of Iran obey your orders,
This is my prayer to the Almighty days and nights.

Fetdah

Iran and Turan are now under your rule,
Now rejoice at your reign, Fetdah,
All the Turkmen people will live happily in the desert,
Know this: do not shed the blood of the innocent, Fetdah.

Today you are a Shah, but you can become a beggar tomorrow,
Deprived of your people, motherland and religion,
One day will come: your soul will leave your body, you will be dead,
You have committed so many sins, Fetdah.

I am sure of it, but if you find it out, you will behead me,
Or will chain me and throw me into a deep trench,
I am telling the truth, you will be adding more sins,
If you continue killing, Fetdah.

You made the Turkmen suffer,
You filled my beautiful land with blood,
Those who are killed in honor have risen from the graves,
You will have to forget your throne, Fetdah.

The people`s revenge is great, your fate is wretched,
You will surely either die or be imprisoned,
Don't hope for life, if you lose your throne,
Because you turned our bread into poison, Fetdah.

The people were plundered because of your order,
You are guilty for the tears, pouring from innocent eyes,
The tender backs were whipped forty times on your order,
Blood was flowing as rivers in front of our eyes, Fetdah.

You separated us from our fathers, mothers, brothers,
You bereaved us of hands, legs, beards and hair,
Teeth, tongues, minds and consciousness,
You turned this world into a prison, Fetdah.

We are separated, our beloved are left behind with tears in their eyes,
Our moaning filled the entire universe,
Your gallows are filled with people hanging,
You hired hundreds of butchers, Fetdah.

Pyragy, nothing is left but sharing and suffering pain
Until Fetdah satiates his thirst for blood,
This makes me feel dead, though I am alive,
If Fetdah finds out about this destan, I will be dead.

Made It Worthless

I've ruined my bright life with grief and sorrow,
The wretched fate has made my efforts worthless,
Fate took by floods the books I'd written;
I could do nothing but cry after them.

Unexpected enemies surrounded us,
All our peers were scattered about;
The book we'd written for five years,
Was obliterated by the Kizilbash tribe.

Some of us have become slaves, our hands tied,
Some were left behind in sorrow and sadness,
Some were sold for profit,
Everyone was given a certain price.

Wretched fate mercilessly put me to endless cries,
The shine of my face faded away from tears,
My manuscript was taken away by the flood,
Turning the ruthless river into my enemy.

Some were left all alone,
Some won't get enough food,
Some won't feel enough grief,
Days and nights turned into a whimper.

Wretched fate's torment will scorch,
Don't take its word for granted, its devotion is forged,
Magtymguly, nothing is wrong with this word,
Fate has bent my straight stature.

Confront Destiny

Endless fear put us into a miserable state,
Let's confront destiny whatever it might be,
Our head is overwhelmed with thoughts,
Don't hinder, let them spread around.

Initially Jepbar created everything from scratch,
Some were created from light; most from soil,
My friends, we've got a message from near and far,
For us to be ready to show heat to the enemy.

Neither old nor young should stay widows,
Turkmen, don't become gossip for others,
Let the enemy be slaves for all Muslims,
And others be taken towards Sonu Dag mountains.

You witnessed the majority become poor,
Some lost their way, some lost their lives,
Oh, dear friends, only God can help you,
Let Ali pull out his Zulpukar, the sword.

No innocent blood should be spilled anymore,
No more children, women, or bread should become the enemy's share,
Remember, our soul is given temporarily,
If God wants it, it will leave us.

Enemies reigned over us,
Many faithful Muslims suffered much,
Our sons and daughters were disparaged,
Let's put an end to all of this.

Pyragy will address the Turkmen people,
Never allow the enemy to ruin its beauty,
My friends, before we are drowned in the flood of the Last Day,
Let the enemy be defeated.

No Choice but to Suffer

Oh, my dear friends, Muslims,
We had no choice but to suffer,
Despite the hard work we've done,
We had to confront the torment.

This world is wide, too much evil,
My sweet life is burning between the two,
A merciless ruler is reigning over us,
We had to attack him at last.

Goklen Khan became loose,
They are envious of our state,
They have taken all our wealth,
So we had to guard against them.

Magtymguly, don't spare your life!
Tighten your belt; put your armor on,
This cruel khan went beyond the limit,
We had no choice but to trap him at last.

In Search of

My country is Etrek, my people are Goklen,
I am in search of love,
My soul is filled with turbulence,
I am in search of the Sufi leader to bless me with power.

I am far from my parents,
From my motherland, the iris of my eyes,
Losing life is easier than separation,
I am in search for a market to sell my goods.

Mammetsapa is my brother,
Mullah Mati is my classmate,
If Abdullah returns, my dear sibling,
I am in search for the Prophet's blessing.

There is so much grief deep in my heart,
Blood filled my eyes, flowing down,
Fate is not a friend to trust,
I am in search of the grave to escape.

Sonu Dag, my pride,
I walk atop your peak,
I am a hunter hunting for mountain deer,
I am in search of a black shiny snake.

Magtymguly, this world,
Brought so much sorrow and grief.
Oh, my Turkmen nation! Oh, all mankind!
I am in search of a free-flowing stream and a ford to cross.

Azady—My Teacher

I entered my inner soul and noticed a sign that bothered me,
Either separation or loneliness is left, my teacher, Azady.

He ran away from the wind, wanting solitude,
After nine years of appeal, he became my brother, my Azady.

Always dashing around, he deprived me of my will,
He locked his garden, his flowers are faded, know this, my Azady.

What is this? Why all this sorrow? The sun and water are crying.
My never-ending tears have become more eager, my Azady.

In search of remedy for my pain, Lukman wandered from country to country,
His fame spread all over the world, my teacher, Azady.

Just wait and see, the whole world will be aware of my pain,
I am afraid this world is tired of me, my Azady.

Pyragy says, father, just have a look at my pain,
Otherwise I am losing my will, my patience is gone, my Azady.

My Son—My Azady

Azady: Reveal your secret, don't dare to hide it,
But, please, follow my advice, my son!
Hundreds of thoughts come to my mind every day,
Don't break my heart, don't make me suffer, my son!

Magtymguly: I am ashamed to reveal my secret,
But if you ask me, I'll disclose it, my Azady!
Hundreds of thoughts come to my mind every day,
I wish to join you in a journey, my Azady!

Don't suffer, ask the Almighty for your rescue,
Don't dream of becoming either a khan, a beg or a sultan,
What God gave us should be enough,
Don't be deceived; don't go away, my son!

Never did we travel in six or five,
If we travel much with many peers,
Maybe then my sad heart will be pleased,
The joy will fill my soul, and won't calm down, my Azady.

You have no experience, you are young, and you can't go,
There would be sleepless nights, and storms on the way you'd not endure;
You won't succeed in every work you've gotten yourself involved in,
Don't try to leave me, my son!

The secret is not revealed if it is not shared;
A young man does not tell good from bad.
If you don't let me go this time, my soul won't be pleased.
Don't make me change my mind; let me go, my Azady!

How dare you leave us in such a state?
This path is not a good one, the one you want to go,
I beg you my son, please, come, don't go,
Don't get into mischief and losses, my son!

I have a great desire to get to know Islam,
The people expect only money: tenge and dirhem.
Don't make my soul sad, don't beg me,
It is only once you are given a chance, please, let me go, my Azady!

You'd better always read the Quran; it will show you the right path,
Afghan people are cruel, but their belief is Islam,
The roads are full of villains, dissolute and wicked,
You might be killed, or get lost; don't go, my son!

Let me test my fate today,
I will know whether my fortune prepared a good day for me,
If death comes in search of my soul,
It will find me wherever I am, even here, my Azady.

Where will you go with such a purpose?
What a deed is it that you insist on so much?
Tell me at last, who are you going with?
Don't hide your eyes, sighing deeply, my son!

I am ready to become an aide for Yazyr Khan,
Poor man, his spirits will be high,
This is the seventh day that I have been reading the sura "Alham" from the Quran
Make my heart happy, let me go, Azady!

Azady says: let's enjoy this life together,
Well, I will let you go, let you try your fate,
Stand up my son and say "Amen," I will bless you,
Let God be your companion, my son, go then!

Magtymguly says: staying behind I lose a lot,
My dream calls me from afar,
Wherever you are ask God for my health,
Reading prayers beg Almighty to pardon me, my Azady!

My Father

In the Year of the Fish, at the age of sixty five, on Nowruz Day,
The angel of death came and blocked the life path of my father,
This is the order of this world, that is true;
Death struck and cut the string of my father's life.

He never wished for excessive wealth,
He was never fond of old joy and the fun of this world,
He never wore anything except old sack cloths,
His only wish was to have a place in the Afterlife.

He used to say: this world will not stay, no one is granted an eternal life,
Fasting during the day, spending nights awake,
He was free of doubts, the true believers are certain,
My father earned respect worthy of the Prophet's support.

I won't say anything purely based on a guess, unless I see it with my eyes,
He who truly believed will reach his goal,
My father's tomb will not be unguarded,
Both angels and jinns will fulfill this job.

Sultans said three hundred saints were seen,
I caught sight of my father amongst forty pirs,
As I approached them he was amongst the seven prophets,
My father truly was one of the Abdals.

A person never stays in this world; only his fame remains after him.
The humankind of this world neglect these truths,
My father's body lies in his grave in peace,
His home is Paradise, his soul is happy.

Magtymguly, you hide a secret in your soul,
If you find a worthy man, do not spare your efforts to serve him,
Whoever is a true friend of my father, will be granted
His worthy place in Paradise on the Day of Judgment.

Where Is My Azady?

I was in search of fate, but it confronted you,
The light of my eyes—where is my Azady?
You took my heart and gave it to the mutts,
The sultan of my soul—where is my Azady?

My mosque and mihrab are left without the imam,
My moon didn't rise and didn't shine,
I was left alone, the flood surrounded me,
The ocean of my soul—where is my Azady?

My sweet words turned into a bitter poison,
My face turned yellow like saffron,
Weakness seized me, my eyes darkened,
Azan of my pulpit—where is my Azady?

My four seasons turned into the fires of hell, the mountains melted,
The living flew away, the dead started to walk,
Everyone who was left met with God,
The tongue of my people—where is my Azady?

The soil turned into mudflow, the mudflow turned into sand;
Large pots turned into bowls, whereas bowls into large pots;
My joy turned into mourning, anguish is my only lot;
Peace of my heart—where is my Azady?

The dead rose and begged the Almighty,
They went and repeated only one word to God,
Pleading much, "Let him go," —they said,
Joy of the dead and the living—where is my Azady?

Infidels wept, and accepted Islam,
Hydyr and Solomon begged God,
The ocean turned into vapor to reach heaven,
The hero of the Goklen—where is my Azady?

I wish for nothing but to fight you, Fate,
Either you win and I shall be defeated, or I behead you,
I shall feed you to the mutts or sell you at the market,
The basil of my garden—where is my Azady?

The ears that heard this all became deaf,
All mountains melted, stones turned into sand,
Mullahs were left without the Quran, pirs became blind,
The Quran of the rulers—where is my Azady?

You covered the earth with black mist,
Fate, confess who was blessed with your mercy?
Look, you deprived Pyragy of his faith,
The faith of my dignity—where is my Azady?

Don't Leave This Land

Oh, my brother Abdullah,
Don't leave this land,
Let God bless you with strength!
Don't let loneliness be part of your soul.

If you leave this motherland,
Listen to your heart.
If you happen to cross over that ocean,
Maybe the Prophet Noah will come to your aid.

I shall be left behind alone,
And only evil will be my companion,
Each thought of you will make me cry,
My kiblah, my father Azady.

Lofty mountains covered with fog,
Great times pass by,
Trees are abundant with fruit,
Hiding you, the gardener.

What fate has given us!
It took the soul out of my body.
Great nations have fallen ill.
God, send us Lukman, the healer.

I couldn't bear the fathers' whimper,
I couldn't tour the world like a wind,
I couldn't swim in the depths of the ocean,
I disturbed the waters of the Jeyhun.

My elder and younger brother,
My lonely life comes to an end,
Futility became my best friend,
You turned this world into a prison.

My friends, where is my companion?
Those who toured to India,
Those who saw the light of God's countenance,
Did you see Hanmengli?[6]

I constantly entreated favor,
I constantly caused my soul misery,
I was foully slandered,
I faded as if in a cold fall.

I cried over injustice, my bloody tears flowing,
The loneliness seized my heart;
My word is not worthy of trust,
I should forget that God.

Everything is turned upside down,
The soil turns into oil,
With whom shall I share my grief?
To whom shall I reveal this secret?

I didn't see such a pristine land,
I sacrificed a lot,
A gamesman became my companion,
While travelling in India.

I was fooled by a healer,
Foxes and jackals acted as leopards,
All mullahs became avid,
And forgot the Quran.

I will speak if you ask me to,
My flame will sting if you come close,
If you go to the house of the rich,
They won't welcome you as a guest.

Crabs wonder in the ocean.
Travel the world whenever you can!
You do not know when your breath will stop;
Not until God orders it so.

A word came to my tongue,
I wore a belt around my waist,
Magtymguly says: I dedicated,
All destans to my people.

Abdullah

Nine years passed since the day you left,
Where is your homeland then, my brother Abdullah?
He who once left would return, wouldn't he?
Where is your homeland then, my brother Abdullah?

I waited for news from you, kneeling in front of the mountains;
But only silence comes in return, no word of you,
Stranded alone, apart from your parents, how do you get by?
Where is your homeland then, my brother Abdullah?

Fear cannot help if one's soul is destined to leave,
Life came to an end, time is up.
Or were you swallowed by the ocean's depths?
Where is your homeland then, my brother Abdullah?

We have been covered with the curtain of separation.
My strength left me bending my knees.
Crying his heart out, my father lost his stature.
Where is your homeland then, my brother Abdullah?

I pleaded for news before all living creatures,
But I had to surrender to inevitable separation,
No more can I tolerate such an endless sobbing,
Where is your homeland then, my brother Abdullah?

There is no relief for me amongst my people,
My sufferings added to the pains I had,
Abandoning your motherland and your beloved,
Where is your homeland then, my brother Abdullah?

I am keen on listening to every uttered word,
This separation is torturing us all,
I am brave enough to throw myself into the fire.
Where is your homeland then, my brother Abdullah?

No time was spent in joy and fun together,
You left early, abandoning us all.
Magtymguly is torn by tears over this bitter loss.
Where did you make your home, brother Abdullah?

The Trace Is Found

I lost all hopes thinking that Abdullah is gone for good,
But merchants came and brought me back my hope,
Seeking to meet him I wandered the hills like Mejnun,
All in vain, my sad heart was full of despair.

My empty thoughts were filled with sorrow,
My eyes closed, my brows became heavy.
My fellow friends who used to recite the Quran,
Forgot how to pray in search of wealth.

I lost my stature, what should I do?
My clothes faded and there was no way to kill my thirst,
Tell me what brought me to this life of Mejnun,
Stranded away from my people and my land.

My fate has set me on fire.
Striving to burn the sparks of beauty on my face,
All I had turned into ashes in my efforts
To erect a fortress, because of Satan's victory over me.

The waiting birds were almost choked in a cage;
Horses are bursting and jumping into action.
Getting lost I found myself in the street of love;
Convoys came, putting an end to my zeal.

Magtymguly, all those who came to greet me,
Passed by on their horses,
My fellows all headed for pilgrimage to Medina,
Leaving me all by myself, apart from my friends.

Perished[7]

My sister-in-law Bayram, my sister Hanmengli, Janesen,
I don't know which of you I should mourn,
Wretched fate, you turn to the left every day,
The world of my heart has perished.

The fate of three people you trampled down to earth,
I wasted my life with grief and sorrow,
Night after night I prayed for God's mercy,
Even the sky started crying seeing my grief.

Magtymguly, my graceful stature has bent
My veins have gotten tense; my blood has stopped flowing,
Death struck me from three directions,
My mind is blurred, I am lost.

Where Are You?

What should I do, he whose throne is ruined, my Suleyman where are you?
I almost spared my soul, my only belief; where are you?
The owner of my throne and crown, oh my sultan, where are you?
The iris of my eyes, the one blessed by God, where are you?
My beloved mother, my Mecca Medina, my precious one, where are you?

No smile touched your face for the sufferings brought to you by this fate,
Never did you take me in your hands, saying: oh, my poor boy,
Never did you grant a look of passion filling joy at my celebrations,
Never did you stop to inquire what fate sent to me,
My beloved mother, my Mecca Medina, my precious one, where are you?

If I tell all what I feel looking at this world,
Will I find you, my precious beauty, if I go in search for you?
If I go to the desert, and weep there days and nights,
If I look for you in this world abandoning everything else,
My beloved mother, my Mecca Medina, my precious one, where are you?

I didn't see your flower-like face due to the fate,
She was unaware of the fate's chosen path because of all her mourning,
She left this world and freed herself from the troubles,
Oh, and now I do not notice spring, Nowruz or winter passing by.
My beloved mother, my Mecca Medina, my precious one, where are you?

I might be blind not to notice the sufferings you endured,
My face turned into black with shame among whole communities.
My sweet words turned into poison today;
My mountains turned into deserts, my plains turned into mountains,
My beloved mother, my Mecca Medina, my precious one, where are you?

Being left alone in this world my soul will be filled with turbulence,
Without you I am a poor man, what do I have to do, a poor thing?
This world lost its value and became a prison for me,
If I roam like a sheep, will I find a sign?
My beloved mother, my Mecca Medina, my precious one, where are you?

Oh, father, the sun turned into blood not being able to tolerate this pain,
The fate might get into a fight with your dearest soul,
Bloody tears were flowing like a flood from my eyes,
I swallowed the deadly poison and the final clothes were put on me,
My beloved mother, my Mecca Medina, my precious one, where are you?

If I faced it now I would definitely fight it,
My heart suffered so much due to the separation, granted by the wretched fate,
Severe winds blow away the blossom, the garden is completely emptied,
God will not hear my complaints, my heart is on fire,
My beloved mother, my Mecca Medina, my precious one, where are you?

The mountains and rocks will cry along the mud streams,
The rivers of Amu Darya and the Nile appealed to Almighty God,
Look, a nightingale was captured in a garden by a hyacinth,
My father Azady is crying—together with my people, Goklen and Yomut,
My beloved mother, my Mecca Medina, my precious one, where are you?

Your beautiful moon left this transient world to the eternal life,
Your palace is abandoned by its Sultan, can't keep its tears.
The string of my bow broke off, and it is worthless without its arrows.
I am telling the truth, and it might be that your place is in paradise,
My beloved mother, my Mecca Medina, my precious one, where are you?

Magtymguly says: I completed this destan,
And I, your poor child, climbed the mountain and cried.
I thought of the Creator, knowing he will be my remedy on the Day of Judgment,
Not a single person is left in this world whom I did not ask,
My beloved mother, my Mecca Medina, my precious one, where are you?

Where Are You My Faith?

Oh, what should I do, my dearest, where are you?
My companion in two worlds, my faith, where are you?
The light of my eyes, the brightest ray, where are you?
What is the Garden of Paradise for me, my heavenly moon, where are you?
My mother, my Mecca Medina, where are you?

Oh, due to the severity of fate the soul abandoned the body.
Her soul separated and left to the city of Paradise.
Oh, the tops of the mountains have freed themselves from the mist mixed with rain,
Oh, today woke up with grief having dried the ocean,
My mother, my Mecca Medina, where are you?

I couldn't see her flower-like face in that eternal world as much as I wished,
With tears in both her eyes she said: "I didn't see the light,"
"Pyragy, Pyragy!" —She called, forgetting her further words,
When she put herself into suffering within the soil against her will,
My mother, my Mecca Medina, where are you?

Even the partridge wouldn't leave her child in the desert,
The nightingale always cries, revealing her grief to the universe,
What can a mountain deer's fawn do when it is out of its mother's care,
Bad luck does not have any shame; it subjected us to a separation,
My mother, my Mecca Medina, where are you?

Kings will abandon their throne if they have no people,
If you put a tree into fire, it will burn and turn into ashes,
If you destroy a beehive, they will gather and fly away,
If a yeanling dies in the presence of his mother, the mother wouldn't be able to bear it,
My mother, my Mecca Medina, where are you?

The cattle will be gathered and given to a shepherd,
If the shepherd is sleeping, the cattle will certainly scatter around,
Every time they will run into a jackal, leaving none alive.
Oh my friends, I have encountered such an end to the world
My mother, my Mecca Medina, where are you?

The entire nation moaned wishing to see you,
The spring disappeared turning into winter,
Clouds rained heavily getting angry with my state,
The mudflow will rush like an ocean, overflowing the whole world,
My mother, my Mecca Medina, where are you?

Suddenly I found myself in the garden and saw my flowers faded,
My nightingales died not from the blade, but from the fire of hell,
The river burst its banks and flooded the whole world,
The entire nation of mine is crying, marking the day of mourning,
My mother, my Mecca Medina, where are you?

Look, today a brave, young man dropped his sword,
He can't find a way out in this vast and endless world,
The cypress tree suddenly lost all its leaves,
All my uncles, her brothers and sisters are moaning and crying badly,
My mother, my Mecca Medina, where are you?

Having lost my dear mother, I called myself Pyragy,[8]
I forgot everyone, family and friends, even a single thing that once belonged to me,
The robber cast an eye and captured my most precious diamond today,
The mountains fell into pieces not being able to bear my flaming grief,
My mother, my Mecca Medina, where are you?

Parting

I lost the shine of my eyes, parting with my dear soul,
The throne of my happiness ruined, departing from the kingdom of this world,
The flowers of my garden withered, losing the fragrance of its amber and basil,
After we lost our great fighter, an enemy started to fight,
I lost my patience, parting with my beloved.

No one will be able to rescue me as I am an unfortunate poor servant,
Water is greatly valued by fish, but I am like a flood not wanted by anyone,
The poison is the food for living creatures, but I am the honey mixed with poison,
I am like wretched flower that separated from its nightingale,
I lost my patience, parting with my beloved.

All who lost their close ones will cry; their moaning will reach the seventh layer of Heaven,
Look how this fate grasped and enslaved a poor servant like me,
Fate disgraced me, playing her ill will on me,
It gave the order of death to me sending me to the city of separation,
I lost my patience, parting with my beloved.

What I chose to be good led me to misfortune,
What I chose to be a horse to saddle, turned out to be a donkey,
What this fate sent as its rays to me dropped to the earth as poison,
Even the city of Yemen cried taking mercy of my state,
I lost my patience, parting with my beloved.

I lost the sight of her soul as if it were spring rain,
I lost my patience and hastened to see what fate had there for me,
Seeing what ills my fate prepared for me, I repented, oh Lord, take my life,
Not realizing the outcome, I threw myself into the fire,
I lost my patience, parting with the beloved.

The Almighty won't listen to my pleas, I have no way out, my dear friends,
My entire body is on fire, but look, no wounds are seen.
You subjected me to severe sufferings; even fate has lost its count.
Pyragy says, what an injustice, there is no end to this separation,
I lost my patience, parting with the beloved.

Ill-Starred

What a disaster, what a sorrow, what chaos,
No one takes mercy on me, I'm ill-starred,
Even if I moan my wishes won't be heard by the Almighty,
No one takes mercy on me, I'm ill-starred.

My fate befriended the others,
It wouldn't listen to my complaints, even when I shared them.
It sent my people over the mountains and valleys,
No one takes mercy on me, I'm ill-starred.

I lost my courage just like Görogly,
Having become old, I lost my power,
I lost my sons, dear to me as my two eyes,
No one takes mercy on me, I'm ill-starred.

I spent my nights and dawns with no sleep,
My heart is on alert and my soul is not at peace,
My father, mother and brothers all passed away,
No one takes mercy on me, I'm ill-starred.

He, who met his ill fate, can't run away,
He, who has an arrow, won't be shot,
A man, who is alone, will never be remembered,
No one takes mercy on me, I'm ill-starred.

My friends got engaged in various crafts,
They went far away, and separation split us,
My wishes and dreams turned into sorrow,
No one takes mercy on me, I'm ill-starred.

Every day I have to confront my evil fate,
Who will provide support for my poor soul?
Now evil people will seem good to me,
No one takes mercy on me, I'm ill-starred.

My shepherd got lost, and sheep got scattered around,
My destiny has become evil, I lost my dream,
My aged self turned sixty,
No one takes mercy on me, I'm ill-starred.

I surrender myself to grief, I lost my mind,
My palace is ruined; I let my caravan go,
I've even forgot my love, my beloved Mengli,
No one takes mercy on me, I'm ill-starred.

This world has become cold to many people,
The poor turned into beggars, not being considered men of honor,
Cowards got courage and became rulers of the people,
No one takes mercy on me, I'm ill-starred.

Oh, what do I have to do, I wasted my youth?
The trees of my garden died, it became desert,
The fog had vanished, my mountains had melted,
No one takes mercy on me, I'm ill-starred.

Magtymguly, I am unable to come to my senses with all these tears,
Whatever I owned is lost, my shop is empty,
My honor and dignity are trampled,
No one takes mercy on me, I'm ill-starred.

I'd Like to Feel the Wind of Dawn

I'd like to feel the wind of dawn,
On the hills of Dehistan,
I'd like to see Zengi Baba,
Bahauddin, Mirkulal.

The one whose clog is the crown of the heavens,
The one whose name is well known in the Universe,
The one who is needed in both worlds,
I'd like to see the one, who speaks Arabic.[9]

Whoever comes won't stay long likewise dawn,
Their time spent in apologies won't be long,
A soul desires to travel a lot,
In order to see the world.

I'd like to see good and bad,
Like Hydyr in deserts,
Like Ilyas in waters,
Like Kowus in mountains.

I'd like to see India located up on the map,
Turkestan, which is behind on the map,
I'd like to see the Roman Empire,
The ocean of the cemeteries.

The soul is crazy, the world is wild,
What won't be of use in it?
Seven mountains, seven rivers,
I'd like to see the entire wild world.

If Magtymguly is happy,
If tears fill my eyes,
If my faith is my companion,
I'd like to go to see the Kaaba.

With the Stones

My heart will say, "I'd like to go far from people,
To walk in the mountains and stones."
Recalling all my sins and wrongdoings,
I'd like to wash my face with my tears.

I see that everybody is engaged in something.
My heart is preoccupied with sorrow,
I'd like to sit in a remote corner,
Under the trees with my head full of thoughts.

An old world is full of deception,
Humankind is full of dreams,
The world is full of conflicts,
Every person faces hundreds of problems.

Inspired people are in love with God,
The strong and capable won't meet,
The soul is not at ease, my friends,
One hundred remedies won't calm it down.

I spent a lot of time in thoughts,
But I don't know what I achieved with this,
I lost my path being preoccupied with my thoughts,
I wasted all my time with lazy ones.

Don't waste your life for trifles,
If we wake up the quiescent fate,
Reading prayers at dawn,
I would like to share my laments with the birds.

Magtymguly, if I am granted support,
To find a worthy man to serve him,
The heart will say: "I'd like to be,
A companion to preaching dervishes."

Oh, Beys, My Time Has Passed

Oh beys, at dawn I passed a path
Through the tall mountains,
Oh beys, I walked by torrents
Once seen by the saints.

Oh beys, I saw geese resting in the lakes,
Listened to the pleasant melodies,
Embraced young women and girls,
With so much pleasure and joy.

Oh, beys, crossing my land on the back of a gray horse,
I enjoyed the fragrance of sweet basil in the morning,
I have shared with the poor
All the gold and silver taken from the shop.

Oh beys, travelling with good intention in my heart,
I never got off from my horse of wealth,
I emptied forty bowls of sweet waters
From the spring of Köwser.

Oh beys, being a wretched man I was wandering around crying,
My heart was burning with fire,
Look! Now I have wings raised and
I have reached the skies.

Oh beys, covering myself with the mud of Köwser,
Like an arrow to the bow of your eyebrow,
I hope the time will come, when
I reach my beloved, at her place in Paradise.

Oh beys, the people who came here will ask about me,
The people whom I taught will be grateful to me,
At the age of twenty
I suffered much from love.

Pyragy says, I am like an arrow,
Look, as a palace in this world,
Oh beys, look and know that today
With time passing, I set down like the Moon.

The Days That Became Old

Old mountains, have a look
At the days that grew old like you.
Take away from me your tops,
Those days of my life full of sufferings.

I am separated from my parents,
I am a dried out well,
I am the spring that came with no desire,
Those days that ruined all my dreams and desires.

Being separated from Abdullah and Mammetsapa, I have suffered a lot,
Having separated from them,
There is no devotion from this world,
Those days when all my efforts were in vain.

I didn't have a chance to enjoy a son or a daughter,
I never took a spear into my hands.
I so much wish to go to Tovriz,
Those days when each of my steps was cursed.

Magtymguly, I have no patience,
I am praying to you my Lord,
My tribe of Goklen is at unrest,
The days when they encountered their enemy.

Challenged by Fate

My friends, brave young men,
Everyone is challenged by fate,
God granted each his own path,
Everyone desired to fulfill his duty.

Some took the path of God,
Only good deeds were their intention,
Some took swords into their hands,
They fought and paved the way for Islam.

Beys and khans with thoroughbred horses and camels,
Will fill the plains when all of them saddle,
They destroyed the shields, shed the blood,
The brave men lost their heads.

We were in need of a strong ally,
But instead we got surprised,
Some went to Iran, Turan
Some crossed over to Esfahan, Tovriz.

God was aware of my state,
But people might not know for sure,
Magtymguly, my path was
Separated from that of my friends.

I Reached That Age

As I got older, I lost my conscience,
Oh, friends, my age reached fifty.
Oh Kareem, my fear is disappearing day by day,
This ill intention of mine got firmer with every breath.

Unfortunately, I did nothing for religion,
My life is full of suffering, my beard became gray,
My strength is weakened, my teeth are blunt,
But I still dream that I am young.

My heart always was in search of the world's gold,
My eyes too always looked for the beauties,
My tongue too always was in gossip and lies,
Satan is an infidel, greed is all cruelty.

If help doesn't come in time from you, oh Jabbar,
When will there be a chance to overcome this disaster?
I was attached to illusory dreams and desires,
Not having the slightest capability to serve God.

Friends, I have no trust in this life,
My destiny is blacker than coal,
The sun of my fate is covered by mist,
My Lord, please, awaken my sleeping fate.

Oh, Allah, my true greed might be awful,
But my wish from the Gracious is the light of faith,
My bad deeds are innumerable, as well as my sins,
Please, I beg you to forgive me, oh my Zuljalal.

Magtymguly, I am on fire with love,
If others grieve for their property, I am in misery because of my state,
I am wandering between my fears and hope,
My Lord, what will become of me on Judgment Day?

Withered Due to Moaning

Oh, my life, oh, my sweet life,
It withered due to moaning.
My soul and body burnt down
Due to the flaming fire.

Oh, my life, oh, my black eyes,
Who would need my words?
I am the only one among Goklen,
Who has been left with dreams unfulfilled.

Oh, my life, oh, my flourishing spring
Will no longer be seen by my eyes,
Magtymguly, all my pain and sufferings,
Have gone with my body and soul.

What Should I Do, Now I Am Wretched?

I was a khan in my motherland,
I could deliver orders to khans,
I was a remedy for sickness,
I was a provider for the poor,
I was a source of life for the lifeless,
What should I do, now I am wretched?

I was eyes for the blind,
I was a tongue for the dumb,
I was a source of respect for my nation,
I was a whim for the loved ones,
I was Hatam Tay himself,
What should I do, now I am poor myself?

I was sweet basil in the Garden of Eden,
I was a source of gold in my motherland,
I was a gracious horse for the brave men,
I was a haze on top of the mountains,
Pyragy says: "I was safe and sound,
But now I am a palace in ruins."

No Fame Is Left Behind

Due to the cruelty of fate,
The lovers lost their fame,
Due to the cruelty of soil,
Neither life, nor anything was left behind.

Fate is the cause of all disasters,
Unhappiness is the result of fate's way,
The brave men's council decayed,
The Community at large ceased its being.

What a torture has been brought by fate,
Sweeping the spirits of my soul and the brightness in my face away
Since everyone has become "smart,"
There was no more demand for the adviser's art.

Fate, stop seeking reasons,
You, the inflictor of torment to the poor and rich,
Guests are not welcomed anymore,
And elderly are not respected.

The torrents are trapped on mountain slopes,
My mind is lost and my spine is curved,
Magtymguly says: "oh, people of my land,
I have no descendants to leave after me."

Will Search For

Being drowned in the mud of sufferings due to separation,
My sleep deprived eyes will search for the peaceful land.
A nightingale, which spent too many years in the cage of moaning and howling,
Will search for red flowers when freed.

My beloved land, I will cover; long distances searching for you,
My eyes are filled with sand, my state is wretched,
Neglected and worn out weirs by the river banks,
Will search for oceans and floods, shedding their tears.

The passion of souls dressed in burning clothes,
The thrones and palaces left without rulers,
Poor lovers wandering around in search of their beloved,
Will search for their tall beloved with dark eyes and slender waist.

Impatient souls, incapable bodies,
If blood of the innocent people is shed,
They will be flying like butterflies over the spring flowers
And will search for early morning wind in the spring.

Speechless mouths, ugly faces,
Black eyebrows, arrow like eyelashes, those black eyes,
Inappropriate talks, meaningless words,
They will go beyond the secret places, and will search for the deaf and dumb.

Stupid kings, powerless viziers, those slaves,
Slim waists, tall like cypress trees, white and long arms,
The tracery of the soul, wishes seen in dreams,
They will look for gold, diamonds, pearls, treasures and wealth.

Magtymguly, both poor and rich,
Bows with no arrows, and no strings,
The time, the days and months that passed,
The time will move forward searching for a new year.

The Good Times Have Not Come

I am an ignorant one; I got trapped by fate,
I have been waiting long, but the good times have not come,
And now I can't bear the departure,
I have been waiting long, but the good times have not come.

I am nearly forty, and my bowl is full,
Having gone through a lot of pain in vain, I am not happy,
My good intention has turned to be a bad companion for me,
I have been waiting long, but the good times have not come.

A severe disaster has come and hit the people,
It opened its mouth and licked with its tongue,
It is like a wild dog biting everyone it encounters,
I have been waiting long, but the good times have not come.

A poor man is not respected; he won't be seen in gatherings.
Though he's loved by God, he is not granted wealth;
Even if he rides a horse, he won't walk with his legs bound,
I have been waiting long, but the good times have not come.

Envious people have only one intention—to collect wealth,
Not eating themselves they are strangling the bounty granted to them,
Their riches will become haram, causing lots of problems,
I have been waiting long, but the good times have not come.

The mullahs consider my true words false,
They are ready to support false words instead,
Look, steel has melted under their oath,
I have been waiting long, but the good times have not come.

The pirs have revealed their true faces,
Getting in love affairs with the youth, the shameless ones are,
Considered to be Sufis. They say: "This is what Allah says,"
I have been waiting long, but the good times have not come.

Magtymguly, he who has got fire on his tongue, will spread its flames around,
He won't take mercy and will reveal the misdeeds of an evil man,
If he is given wings by God he will fly to India,
I have been waiting long, but the good times have not come.

The Hasar Mountains

The Hasar Mountains are high,
Their slopes are full of antelopes,
Hunters will find plenty of game there,
If they go to the Hasar Mountains.

The Hasar Mountains have their own paths,
He, who sees them will admire;
You can see the most beautiful women,
If you take a walk in the Hasar Mountains.

A mountain is the sultan of the earth,
It has created a treasury within its slopes,
One should know, the land of three hundred
And sixty saints is in the Hasar Mountains.

Nomads settled down there,
The snakes are in their service,
Everything grows in its valleys,
For those who look for it in the mountains.

The lions and tigers roam there,
Wild mountain deers stealthily looking,
It is difficult to reach its top,
Even if you climb the Hasar Mountains sweating.

Magtymguly says that these mountains
Have been burnt by the fire of love,
If you are in love you will enjoy your time,
Staying in the Hasar Mountains.

Gurgen

There is a big mountain in front of it with a haze on its tops,
The wind of Gurgen blows, coming from the sea,
When the streams are filled with rain due to the heavy clouds,
The mudflows of Gurgen will run steadily.

There are forests of reeds there,
And amazing beauties wearing gold and silver,
Well-fed sheep, racing horses and cows,
These are the animals that make up the herds of Gurgen.

Thoroughbred camels walk in orderly rows,
Loaded with the heavy goods of their wealthy merchant owners,
There are tall and steep overhanging cliffs,
Surrounding it on its front and back, right and left.

There are beys with their embroidered silk belts on,
Riding their horses with falcons in their hands,
There are mountain deers with their white chests enjoying the sea breeze,
And fallow deers bleating in the deserts of Gurgen.

Magtymguly will cross many lands,
Suffering from the pain of separation,
Graceful fairies with eyes resembling the ones of deers will wave,
Walking down the river fords of Gurgen.

Sonu Dag

Sonu Dag, you are our life,
Ash trees make up your green belt,
When seeing invaders coming towards you,
Your people, Goklen and Yomut, are ready to encounter them.

The hope is that we build pasture in Öyluk,
Have horse races and give prizes,
The hope is that we'll reap the harvest of wheat in Temete,
All this is for realizing your dream of sharing food.

Amazing hills will stretch one after another,
The hills covered with wild red flowers will cheer you up,
All various cattle will drink,
Cool water from your spring there.

The vegetation growing there is diverse,
Each settlement will have its own valley,
The caravans will pass one after another,
You are on the path to Naybadai.

Magtymguly, when you speak up,
When this time will pass by you,
When your people will leave their places,
How will they tolerate this state of yours?

This Torment

I have travelled and wandered a lot due to the fire of love,
What a disaster; who is able to tolerate this torment?
If the flame of love is brought to the sky,
Even the skies will shatter under the load of this torment.

The candles won't light up if there are no signs of love,
Even birds and wolves shed tears when in love,
High and mighty mountains droop their heads downward,
Even the stones will melt unable to tolerate this torment.

If there was a brave man who was able to carry this load of love,
Then the fate on seeing that would get scared and turbulent.
When the bowels of the Earth begin to move and shudder,
Even the desert will not survive, unable to tolerate this torment.

Paradise ran away to the highest level of Heaven,
Hell hid deep, scared under the layers of the ground.
The river ran away, taking people along,
For four hundred years this torment has been suffered.

Magtymguly, if you have to tolerate this suffering from the very start,
Do not riot; do not complain about your life.
The death and separation is the custom given us since old times,
This torment is bequeathed to us by our fathers.

Frankly, I Cannot Find Peace

Oh, fairy, I am in love with you and I am on fire, to be frank,
Not seeing your flower-like face, I cannot find peace, to be frank.

I had heard a name of one fairy in your city, your name,
I am your poor nightingale; I am howling and moaning, to be frank.

I am a merchant; I sell goods of love,
I came to your city just as a merchant, to be frank.

I won't dare to go to your city, I am afraid of wantonness and sins,
I remember the words of seven pirs, to be frank!

Oh, fairy, your curls; to be frank, all my desire is to be at the service
Of a beauty like you with all my heart and soul, says Magtymguly.

About My Beloved Mengli

Fate disgraced me, separating me from the one I need,
What can I do to hear about my beloved Mengli?

The earth trembled, causing all living creatures to panic,
Skies trembled as well and stars burned due to the fire burning in my heart.

There was a cruel king who left traces in my heart,
He captured Lukman, he will not come to relieve me from my pain.

He did not visit us even once a day; our grief has overtaken us,
My body turned into ashes, my soul is not finding peace.

If this transient world were a hawk it would not have given its crown,
It will never be ashamed, it will laugh, it will not be afraid of my gaze.

If I put my source of water at her service, I hope she will open it forty times a day,
She will drink the pure water of Abu-Kowser from my spring.

Magtymguly will burn with fire, putting on clothes on fire,
Burning the entire transient world with the fire of your tongue.

I Am Enslaved

My favorite Mengli, I cannot come, fearing your influences,
Having fallen in love with your eyes and black eyebrows, I am enslaved.

Executioners would tie me, a poor servant, with chains,
When there is no support on your behalf, what will become of me?

They'll kill me just like Nesimi was killed, and they will give me to be eaten up by dogs,
And vultures will fight between themselves over my dead body.

My bones, swept by the wind, will be sent to Hell,
Thus my captivated dear soul of mine will end up in Hell.

The Hell fire won't burn me, each strand of hair given to me will protect me,
Hold me in the trap and take me to your black shiny snake-like braids.

Being capable of bolting snakes from the valley, they will become Satan's companions,
So, set me free, my beloved Mengli, don't lead me, a poor man, astray.

Magtymguly, you should take the name of Pyragy,
When you thought that you freed yourself from the snake, you encountered a separation.

Turned into My Companion

My beloved, hiding her flower-like beautiful face, turned my tears into a river,
Disappearing from this world, she made disasters turn into my companion.

I looked in every direction trying to find my beloved,
I have not found her and she ruined my life again.

Sometimes spending my nights and dawns burning and moaning like a phoenix,
Again, my soul in grief was gripped with disaster.

She will not listen to my pleas, she became so ruthless,
Not being interested in my wealth, she made all my efforts to be in vain.

Pyragy is telling about his grief, let it be worthy of trust,
Being burnt by fire from the very beginning instead, she turned me to the eternal life.

He Will Forget Its Way

Hey, my friends, if only Lukman hears about the state of my soul,
The entire Motherland will be abandoned and he will forget its way.

I am moaning throughout the days and nights,
If Karun will hear my crying, he'll forget about his intention.

The black mountains shed endless tears seeing my state,
These tears turn into a vast ocean, in which Noah will sail his Ark.

The army coming with its flag robbed the city of my soul,
I don't know whether he can find a solution to the fate of my motherland.

Tell my beloved that I had been in prison,
Let her free me, a poor servant, by dropping her hair down,

Magtymguly, your name will be known all over the world,
If all people are taken unaware, hide and do not share this wealth.

They Will Shed Bloody Tears

Those, who suffer, will be ashamed at, seeing what pains I am going through,
Not finding any remedy, the healers will shed bloody tears from their eyes.

The lovers at seeing this fire will forget their own sufferings,
Wandering around mountains and valleys, they won't find Mejnun in the plains.

A single strand of my beloved's hair has enslaved all the Muslims,
Infidels wishing justice will follow her moaning.

If Navoi, Nizami, Firdousi hear my moaning,
They will all lose hope and forget the promises they had given.

I am spending my nights groaning, I have no hope in the daylight either,
My insatiable eyes will never have enough of looking at the face of my beloved.

Pyragy, try to be patient and forget the winter season,
He, who forgets this day, will never benefit from the fall.

With Blood

I lost patience with my beautiful life, what do I have to do with my soul?
My sun having settled down has become friends with blood.

The flame of love is so painful; there is no remedy for it,
No remedy will heal the soul once burnt; it will not burn if you burn it anymore.

Due to the turning fate, some are khans, others are beggars,
Some are hoarders, they will store up wealth, hurrying in this transient world.

My heart is on fire, not a single butterfly will come close by,
Magtymguly will have to leave this world with unfulfilled dreams in his heart.

Witnessing

I spent quite a time befriending a coward,
I tolerated all his problems witnessing his deeds.

Once a flower appeared in my garden and blossomed,
And I gave it to a nightingale not knowing what to do with it.

This nightingale was very happy having met this flower,
Not understanding why, I asked many questions about it.

It said: "I am a butterfly, falling into the world of love;
I threw myself into the fire, suffering grief due to this flower."

Satan came and threw the flower into the fire,
Forgetting that the fire can burn, I threw myself into it.

My body and soul all turned into ashes,
The morning breeze blew, and took me up to the sky.

Magtymguly, I was a fool, it's good that I knew nothing,
Or else I would spend my life suffering; I am happy for this fate.

Looking for Grave-Clothes

What does fate do in the market of this transient world?
It will not be looking for any other clothes, but grave-clothes.

It will make blind those capable of seeing, and make speechless the wise ones,
It will leave elderly people lonely by depriving them of their canes.

It will turn the brave into cowards, thus mowing down many of the courageous,
It will leave Muslims lonely by depriving them of their clothes.

The fire of love has been extinguished, what is the guilt of a butterfly?
It separated it, making it shed bloody tears, depriving it from its beloved.

Magtymguly, this old soul of mine is close to sufferings,
I am afraid it will deprive me of my power of speech.

Moon-Like

For me, you are a flower fairy
Your face resembles a fool bright moon.
Filling my astonished mind with haze,
With your embrace recalling a place in paradise.

The gardens are full of saffron,
The rivers and oceans turned into prairies,
My friends look at this transient world,
Reminding us of an abandoned place.

My beloved is a beauty of beauties,
Her beauty is no lesser than that of a fairy,
With her arrow-like eyelashes, and crescent-like eyebrows,
Resembling a bow with the other glance.

If only I could see her face,
If only I could speak with her,
If only I were free to go whenever she calls,
If only my mind would be strong enough to obey me.

Your beauty awakened me,
Cast a glance at the helpless man,
Talk to me, the madman, my love,
With your melody sounding so sweet.

Whenever lakes are full of swans,
Whenever people are blessed with prosperity and wonders,
Whenever deserts turn into blossoming gardens,
Even an Arabian camel will resemble a gracious deer.

We were ready to do everything,
But fate deceived us again,
Vanity of this transient world,
Resembles vicious hypocrisy.

Share with me the wishes of your soul,
And I will be ready to sacrifice my faith and precious life,
The abode of yours, my beautiful fairy
Resembles the sacred Kaaba mosque in Mecca.

Your beauty resembles a full moon,
Concealed by a veil,
Magtymguly, who lost his mind with love,
Resembles a crazy man wandering among his people.

I Won't Dare

My honey is in such a sound sleep,
I won't dare to wake her,
As if I am under her spell,
My tongue is numb, my words are voiceless.

My insatiable eyes never have enough of you,
My heart filled with an eternal desire to serve you,
My insatiable lips can't wait to kiss you,
I am losing my patience to turn this into reality.

Pyragy said: with my feelings concealed,
My friends, I died not yet feeling the joy of this world,
My soul is like a butterfly in my lifeless body,
Wishing to free itself to reach my sweetheart.

Flower-Like

Hey, my friends, the embrace of a worthy beloved,
Resembles a paradise and a flower,
Diamonds are spread around when she speaks,
And her voice is like the song of a nightingale.

The fire of love burnt us all down,
Don't ask anything from me,
My sweetheart's beautiful face,
Resembles the moon and the sun.

How did I bear this suffering and separation?
The distance is far, no way for me to reach her,
With eyebrows penciled as a bow, and almond-like eyelids,
With braids resembling ears of wheat.

Combing your beautiful curls,
You are driving me crazy,
She is a candle and I am a butterfly around it,
I'm on fire; my body is turning into ashes.

Nobody suffers from love like me in this world,
I can't even fill my desire to see her,
Her teeth are pearls and her mouth resembles a flower bud,
Her waist is so thin like a strand of hair.

Her eyes are like daffodils, she is as tall as a boxwood,
Her eyelashes are thick as steel,
A fairy with a slender body, like a cypress,
She is like an endless bunch of flowers.

Two pomegranates adorn her chest,
A pair of birthmarks adorning her ivory face,
The honey streaming from her lips,
Remind one of sweets and delights.

There is much in her attire,
Her dresses always matching,
The color of henna she died her hands with,
Is as red as the color of blood.

Magtymguly, your life is wasted,
With unfulfilled striving to find your beloved,
Sitting there staring into the distance,
You recall a blind man unable to find his path.

Is There Anyone, My Friends?

Is there anyone, my friends, who'd come
Wishing to choose the path of love?
Is there anyone, my friends, who'd feel,
My sufferings if I should share?

I lost my mind, overwhelmed by this love,
All work and trade is neglected,
Is there anyone, my friends, who lost,
His fame and was disgraced in this world?

Sufferings seized me, the fire is burning inside
Weeping and wailing is my only lot,
Is there anyone, my friends, who lost
His mind like me, a crazy man?

Being full of joy in this transient world
You'd lead a life of laughter and play,
Is there anyone, my friends, who died,
Boiling in the cauldron of love?

If a brave man is struck by love,
Even he will turn into powder and dust,
Is there anyone, my friends, who buried
Himself into the torment of love?

I feel the breath of death nearer and nearer,
No longer can I tolerate this burden,
Is there anyone, my friends, who laughed
At me instead of crying?

No matter how hard Magtymguly tries,
Nobody will feel mercy at his tears,
Is there anyone, my friends, who'd been
Robbed on the path of love?

She Will Be Shy

Mengli, my lady, veiling her face with a sleeve,
Expresses her shyness on seeing us.
Stroking her hair and walking with grace,
Expresses her shyness on seeing us.

Beloved, please, listen to what I say,
Your black curls adorn your beautiful face,
Your black eyes, lined with kohl,
Express your shyness on seeing us.

Wearing green and red, my love
No one would guess her dreams,
Charming both the Yomut and Ahal, she
Expresses her shyness on seeing us.

My fate won't react to my call to move on,
There is no wealth to give to you,
My request to show her face,
Will make her turn away, expressing shyness.

Mengli, my lady, give us a chance to meet,
The lady of ladies, my sweetheart,
Pyragy says: my soul and belief would not
Be enough, and she will express her shyness.

My Gaze Falls on You

Thanks to the blessings of the almighty God,
My gaze fell on my beloved,
Drinking wine at the winery,
My gaze fell only onto a man, who lost his mind with love.

Oh, with mihrab-like beautiful fragrant hair,
With a face sacred and attractive as a pulpit,
Oh, with rouge lips like diamonds,
My gaze sank in your beauty's ocean.

Oh, with pure beautiful eyes,
Come and feel the wound in my heart,
Oh, you are the only one to heal my soul,
My gaze sank in your faith, my beauty.

Oh, with bewitching eyes resembling a deer,
With honey and sweets like words,
Oh, with the face like the sun and the moon,
My gaze sank into its light, my beauty.

People would live tending to dreams,
Servants would be pleased to serve you,
Resembling blossoming flower buds,
My gaze fell on the blossoming garden.

With every braid, resembling ears of wheat
Seeing myself as if I were a nightingale,
Oh, you are like a flower of paradise,
My gaze fell onto paradise itself.

You are the only remedy for this pain,
I wish I could suffer only for you,
Magtymguly will say, my dear,
My gaze fell on my beloved.

Ruined

Oh, my dear friends, this crazy world,
Has ruined all my good days,
This sham, this unfaithful world
Has deprived me of my joyful time.

A young man is in need of a beloved first,
An unintelligent man will find no friend,
A brave young man lonely from the start,
Is subject to a trial by cruel fate.

I have no one to hear my sufferings,
My lions and wolves turn into foxes,
My beautiful country turned into ruins,
The Kizilbash devastated it.

My destan has abandoned me,
I feel as if my soul has left my body,
My beloved Mengli with tears in her eyes,
Has set up a fire deep inside my heart.

A strong wrestler is left with no fame,
The time is like this, what can be done?
A young man offering himself,
Has caused pain inside my heart.

Magtymguly, keep your tongue,
They will twist your straight waist,
Don't cause trouble for your people,
All of them showed their trust.

Turned in Pursuit

Hey, friends! My own brother
Turned in pursuit against me.
My beloved wife Mengli,
Hopelessly crying, turned to grief.

The infidels captured Ibrahim, no matter what,
He is in the hands of the ill-intentioned,
They tied him up and threw him into the fire,
Into a blossoming orchard turned on fire.

They gave little, took much,
They turned into evil usurers,
They came putting on many looks,
And many turned to hysterics.

The envious are reigning freely,
Scholars got more spoiled with every passing year,
Forgetting about doomsday,
Everybody turned into usurers.

Ismail sacrificed his son, women became
Shamelessly immoral with every passing year,
With no one willing to work humbly,
An entire nation turned into idlers.

Mountains lived since long ago,
Beautiful buildings were destroyed,
If one day an order comes from Heaven,
An angel Israfil turned into a zurna.

Judges and rulers did not follow the law,
Did not look for the true cause of the problem,
Did not have any mercy for the unfortunate,
They hung, shot and turned into arrows.

Respectable people turned toward ill-intentions,
Mountain tops are covered with clouds,
All those who were cowards are safe and sound,
And brave men descended into disarray.

People do not have even a grain of courage,
Many buildings have turned into ruins,
That racehorse with daffodil-like beautiful eyes
In the hands of cowards became a donkey.

Pyragy, please, stay innocent,
Learn from the strong and the brave,
My sweetheart, come, let's go,
My wonderful native land has turned to grief.

The Time Has Come

What can I do? Aged destiny, my life-long enemy,
Still alive, has come to me.
Let me share with you all my sufferings,
The hair of my head standing on end.

My eyes are deprived of shining luster,
No apples, pomegranates are left in my orchard,
For the sufferings brought by beloved Mengli,
My heart is on fire, boiling and burning.

No longer can I sing and play my music,
If only Allah could hear my melody,
My star has disappeared from sight,
My Moon has set, my Sun is down.

All the offered food is like a poison,
Go and see to be sure our brothers have left,
All friends and trusted ones scattered away,
Crossing over to Iran, Asia and Afghanistan.

The path of Islam is not followed,
No one intends to pursue it,
Magtymguly, imbued with such a passion
Stop it, you are gripped with madness.

Is There Anyone Who Suffered?

Travelers, beggars,
Is there anyone who suffered like me?
The butterflies in search of love,
Is there anyone who had enough of this fire?

Is there any ignorant person in this world
Who has never entered at least one door,
Who has never reached at least one goal,
Who has never had his wit in mind?

You have come like a morning breeze,
Stayed in each house,
Looked around this world,
But is there a fair sultan?

You have no dissatisfaction in this world,
Prophets, speak your mind,
Having once escaped an evil person,
Is there anyone who can escape him forever?

You played a tune on a reed pipe,
I am indebted with many debts,
Is there a bird in this world,
That can escape from the hawks?

Fish, you swim in the ocean,
You stay away from the deserts and steppes,
You swim in many waters,
Is there a place like Paradise?

Fate is not able to seek,
Revolving, it won't limit itself to coming once,
Is there a shop in the market,
Where the goods never end?

Is there a worthy woman in this world,
Who has her speech sweet,
Who has a moon-like face,
Who has an Indian mark on her face?

Secretly, I will tell the morning wind,
Which travels all over the world,
Have you seen my beloved Mengli,
That put my soul on fire?

You used to wander around it,
Near its slope, near where the sun rays fall,
Is there any rain or mist,
On the tops of those aged mountains?

Sitting with his feet in mud,
Burning in fire,
Is there a man brave enough in this world,
Fighting with fate itself?

You travelled days and nights,
Visited many magnificent palaces,
Is there the Quran in those houses,
You visited?

Being by a beauty resembling a cypress,
In the month of Ramadan,
Is there fire and prison,
In the greedy house of this transient world?

Her speech shows her temper,
One can read legends looking into her eyes,
Is there a sign directed toward us,
In the flower-like face of my beloved Mengli?

Magtymguly, you spoke little,
You gave a clear sign of your sufferings,
The geese in the lake flock together,
Is there a Motherland for us?

My Soul Regrets

Zubeyda, my poor, listen to me,
My soul regrets something.
My eyes are bleeding,
Look at the soil; my blood stayed there.

My nightingale, I am suffering.
Happy days of love have passed;
The knife of separation hit me.
My beloved Mengli stayed behind shedding her tears.

The days that passed have turned into a dream,
I wandered around, being ashamed of my people,
Look, my body is emptied;
I feel as if my soul is in the grave.

My sufferings increase with every passing day.
I did not live a happy life in this world;
I worked hard, and suffered much,
The only thing I left behind is the destan I have written.

Cruel fate, unfaithful fate,
You have challenged many souls.
My flower, earth, the sky, an angel,
Oh, my moon-faced beloved stayed behind.

Magtymguly, you feel ashamed,
Nobody will listen to your complaints,
Oh, my Zubeyda, if you fill your eyes with tears,
I left my store behind with no goods in it.

I Am Separated

I'm a nightingale; I am moaning and groaning,
I am separated from my new garden of roses.
Shedding bloody tears from my eyes,
I am separated from my beloved sweetheart.

The stibium looks nice on the eyes of my beloved,
I can endlessly describe her looks,
Her mouth is sweet; her lips resemble a flower bud,
I am separated from the one with black curls.

Alas, my soul is impatient,
My soul takes comfort in her cruelty,
Her eyebrows are furrowed with anger,
I am separated from the one, whose eyes remind those of a blood-sucker?

I am separated from my flower bud,
From my beloved with raven hair,
From my nightingale with a tuneful voice,
I am separated from my sweet-worded beloved.

The dream of my crazy soul,
The queen of all the beauties,
The orchard of the eight layers of the Paradise,
I am separated from this orchard.

Her people and land are amazing,
With cool waters and fresh grass,
She comes from the tribe of Goklen, and her name is Mengli,
I am separated from my tender beloved.

Magtymguly, crazy with love,
Has devoted a destan to glorify it.
Her land of birth is a blossoming garden,
I am separated from its apples and pomegranates.

Shivering

Oh, my friends, my beautiful life,
Is shivering as I grow old.
With sufferings increasing day by day,
It is in need of a remedy.

If a man suffers because of his love,
If a snake catcher looks for the queen of snakes,
If brave men saddle their horses,
Led by their honor and vengeance.

Look, how wise old men,
They have great life experience,
They have seen plenty of good and evil,
Accompanying us all the time.

Magtymguly, you are fifty,
Sadness and anxiety are your friends,
Don't be ignorant, raise your head,
Old age is just a reason for complaints.

Everywhere

The worst thing is living without a beloved,
I wish I had a chance to look around everywhere,
Oh, Creator, grant me a beloved;
I have been suffering greatly.

Send me a beloved with a lovely figure,
A kind soul, with a broad chest,
A sweet speech, clever mind,
With a charming face as well.

Don't drift apart from those who respect,
Don't befriend those who disrespect,
Do not give one, who does not understand,
Let her be modest in her speech and open-hearted.

Your generosity is endless, you know it,
You will say, "Pray, turn to me,"
If you give something, give it faster,
There is no trust in this soul.

Let her be tall, not short,
Let her not be too demanding,
Let her not be stupid, or without manners,
Let her be modest in her speech and open-hearted.

It is not easy to find a good wife,
An ignorant man will not know the value of a good woman,
A man with no wife will have no patience,
If you have the power of Solomon.

Oh, Lord, be merciful, do not leave
Any Muslim with no faith and wife,
Any dervish with no road,
Any young man with no wealth.

Magtymguly, even if I suffer greatly or fall into the fire,
No one will believe me,
I dream of embracing a beloved,
To express my feelings towards her openly.

Today

Venus star rose in the sky,
It is a happy time for a true man in love today.
The flower of the world burst into bloom,
The whole world is full of sweet basil today.

Each time when a nightingale sings its songs,
The flower is iridescent under the wind,
If you are in love, do remember it,
That your beloved is your victim today.

The words are sweet like sugar,
The world is full of flowers,
Your embrace resembles a garden,
Young men want to become gardeners today.

If you want to pick up a bouquet of flowers,
If you want to enter the garden,
If you want to hear news about me,
My tongue speaks like a parrot today.

The mountain tops are covered with mist,
Flowers grow in their valleys,
There is a decree from a fair shah today,
Who defeated a coward at every breath.

The people are a continuation of their brave men,
They won't leave their prey to lions or wolves,
Pyragy's words are like a remedy today,
For the pain of a man who is truly in love.

The Flame of My Beloved

Oh, what shall I do, the flame of my beloved,
Has started a fire in the town of my soul?
I am all surrounded by mist,
My beloved is probably angry.

She might not be part of humankind,
All the fairies of Paradise and young men bow their heads before her,
She is happy, her braids touch us,
I am afraid of the snake -like braids of my beloved.

Diamonds and rubies are on the neck of my beloved,
Even fate cannot help being charmed.
The pomegranates ripened on the chest
Of my beloved are hidden from my eyes.

This is what puts lovers on fire,
The tears of Mejnun have melted,
The fairies of Paradise are
Servants and friends to my beloved.

Oh, old man, the wound of your heart started hurting more,
You, poor man, are the one whom she desires,
Magtymguly—the honor and envy
Of your beloved with no happiness.

Stature

My beloved, when you walk,
I am proud of your cypress-like stature.
An outfit made of flowers,
Fits your wonderful stature nicely.

I am a nightingale suffering because of you,
You have taken my soul as a sacrifice for you,
Let the belt left behind by Zuleyha,
Be fitting for your stature.

My only wish will be fulfilled if I can see your face,
Let my soul freeze in a severe wind,
You are my fate, religion and belief,
I do respect your beautiful stature.

My love for you makes me cry,
I am accustomed to tolerate the pain,
And suffer throughout my entire life,
Over your stature in your night clothing.

He who is in love, will sacrifice himself to see you,
He will abandon his people,
Magtymguly will become a beggar,
For your stature that is like a miracle.

Your Black Eyes

Your executor-like black eyes,
Have become the reason for my soul's burning,
Your executor-like black eyes,
Will have no mercy on me.

My fairy, do not wander all alone,
Don't look at the faces of evil people,
Lining your black eyebrows with stibium,
Your black eyes are like a disaster.

Oh, my Lord, your executor-like eyes,
Have covered the surface of the world with mist,
Have made all the lovers dead,
Your black eyes are at peace.

Magtymguly, the regret for a beloved,
Will make all humans and the manservants of Paradise cry,
The faith and religion for Muslims,
Your black eyes are also sacred.

Playing with the Flower Garden

When I entered the garden of my best friend,
I noticed the sky rise and play with the flower garden.
When I roamed about the foggy mountains,
I noticed two shah's snakes playing and threatening each other.

Two antelopes at the crossing on Köwser spring,
Attracting poor me with pleasant stares;
In the market where the trade of love succeeds,
The seller will haggle and play with the buyer.

I entered the garden, having forgotten the whole world,
I looked at the flower regretfully,
A nightingale was playing with the flower in high spirits,
An apple and a pomegranate, a fig and a pomegranate, are playing.

Good words will find their place on the tongue,
Anything that falls down into the flood won't stay,
Among those of a stable nation, with its courageous men,
Honour and dignity that never get along will play together.

Fate roams around planting the seeds of merciless separation,
So cowards won't get together with the brave,
Magtymguly, having met his beloved Mengli,
Will be having fun with us for five days.

Towards Us

If only we get a chance to set out, God willing,
Wish for the people to move towards us.
If we enter the floods with the support of Noah,
Please, bless us, looking at the ocean.

If only old mountains bow their heads to let us cross,
If the morning wind comes and takes my wishes to my beloved,
If it comes back to bring me a message from my beloved,
And being inspired I write her name into my destan.

My soul is in deep mud due to my old age,
The fate has intentionally sold my destiny,
It closed its eyes, and shot fifty bullets at me,
They came and settled down in my soul.

I'm Mejnun in love for Mengli,
But even she doesn't think how I suffer from it,
Having learned from the love stories of Perhat and Shirin, Zohre and Tahyr,
I have turned into a butterfly myself.

Indian birthmarks like drops of water beautify her flower-like face,
I'm moaning, my groan turned into screaming anger,
Due to long separation my liver is torn apart,
The news about my grief reached even Iran.

Magtymguly, don't forget your nation,
If your tongue seems too long, shorten it.
If your wish is to travel, then tighten your belt,
Merchants will go to Mazanderan.

I Beg for Mercy

Oh, Allah Almighty, the first thing I beg you for
Is that your mercy be sent down to me.
I wish for a beautiful sweetheart,
With almond-like eyes and apple-like cheeks.

What should I do if Allah doesn't bestow this?
Where should I head to, which direction go?
I wish for a beauty with brows seeming pencil-drawn
And very ethical in all her actions.

I wish for a beauty who earned her respect,
One who tends for her husband,
One who never expresses her dislike,
One who has a smile on her face instead.

Twenty years have passed since birth,
But I haven't had any joy in this world,
I wish for a beauty whose words are sweet and whose lips are smiling,
One who is always ready to embrace me.

Magtymguly, your slave, I am here in this world,
I beg for a sweetheart who is smart and clever,
I met an ignoramus, who does not get a hint,
I wish for a beauty who will know my value.

I Have Been Mixed with the Clouds

My smoke has been blown away;
I have been mixed with the clouds.
Fate twisted my arm and spun it around its wheel.
No one came to see me with an interest in their eyes;
The rain of separation started and flooded me with sorrow.

I was gone with the flood of grief and arrived to the country of love,
With my head full of thoughts and mind gone with the wind,
I was standing poor and deprived in the meadow of abundance,
Love plunged with its dagger and tore my heart with separation,
It left me under the sun spreading my destan throughout the world.

There is neither soul nor energy in my dead body,
I'm puzzled and surprised at the same time not knowing what happened,
I am neither sick nor ill, neither dead nor alive,
Sorrow attacked me from the sky when descending,
The fate took me and brought me to the menacing one.

It so happened that mischief attacked and killed me,
Love has taught me the means of this deed,
The fate felt sorry for my hope; it took my hand and lifted it up,
I felt like seeing the appearance of the Almighty,
My friends, I can only speak, for I am torn into pieces.

Magtymguly, my nobility enslaved my beloved,
Having given me a hope, she turned me into a nightingale with a thousand tunes,
The separation put me into the fire; it flamed up and turned me into a whirlwind.
The love flame flared up, it burnt me and turned me into ashes,
Separation, using the one who separates, pushed me to go with the wind.

You Came into Being

One day your father made love,
From that semen you came into being,
From being water first, you turned into blood,
From blood you turned into flesh.

Almighty gave an order for
The seven parts of your body to be in place,
And for your bones to form,
During nine months and nine hours.

God granted you ears and a mouth,
And a tongue in your mouth,
He gave you intelligence and life,
He gave you eyes and brows.

When young, you found a hand,
When you started walking, you found a path,
When you started speaking, you found a language,
When you started eating, you found food.

When you reached seven, you went to school,
You studied and found your life path,
You fell in love with a girl
When you reached fourteen.

You ate and drank what God provided,
You tried different paths in life,
Your beloved loved you in return,
And you two became engaged.

You turned twenty four,
You matured; you were wild as wind,
You raced a horse; you got armed with a sword,
You became capable of fighting in a battle.

When you turn thirty,
Your head is still hazy,
Thanks to the energy of youth,
You wandered and enjoyed life.

You enjoyed your life to its fill,
You witnessed its devotion,
You stepped into your forties,
You are mature now, fully aware.

You couldn't reap all the fruits from the garden of your life,
The frosty wind killed your branches,
You reached that age when
You have to be ashamed of your gray beard at the age of fifty.

You reached sixty now,
Your thoughts are all in despair,
Your happy days are over,
No more springs, winter has come.

At seventy, each time you get on your feet saying "Oh, God,"
You have no strength, you fall;
You are old, you cannot work anymore.
Speak, what are you doing?

If you reach eighty,
How will this state of yours pass by?
The rush and high times are over,
You resemble an abandoned, unharvested field.

At ninety words come out wrong,
The color gray is mistaken for black,
Bones get weaker, and porous,
All you have is one hundred thousand issues.

Magtymguly, your life is gone,
You haven't noticed it as if you were asleep.
What have you done for Allah,
When you reached one hundred?

No Problem

You know, a coward is the one who always answers
Your requests by saying, "No problem!"
If you need to do something urgent,
He will never be found to help you.

He'll twirl his moustache, pulling it to the sides,
He will try to show that his efforts are stronger than a tiger's,
He will roar like a thunderstorm, blasting his throat,
But only after the dish is ready to eat.

He will growl like a lion at the meal,
He will bray like a donkey inappropriately,
Every fox will boast like a lion,
Over the dead bodies.

Don't leave a body in the desert,
Even more so, don't reveal the secret;
Don't exaggerate, stand for your words,
A battle is not a piece of bread on your teeth.

If they say, "Saddle up, saddle up!"
A hyena will eat carefully chewing bones.
When the enemy is close, be braver,
Keep no curse on your beard.

The conscience will never be lost,
It is obvious that a good nature won't be lost either.
These words will not affect animals,
But a man will keep them in his ears.

Magtymguly, there will be a battle,
All secrets of a young man will be revealed.
Brave men will either kill or be killed,
For the sake of their friends.

A Horse Is Needed First

For a young man to earn fame,
A horse is needed first.
To duly welcome guests,
Kind-heartedness is needed first.

A brave man is needed to tolerate sufferings,
A horse is needed to pierce an armoured coat;
To treat people to plenty of dishes,
A welcoming soul is needed first.

Give up all your unrealistic wishes,
There isn't any benefit from wealth.
If time will be against the halal,
The wisdom of the saint is needed.

If you intend to serve God,
To understand the Prophet's path,
To please the souls of dervishes,
Generosity is needed first.

Magtymguly, he is a poor man;
Everything happens according to God's will,
No matter how poor or rich, to those who come,
His welcome is needed first.

Resembles a Horse

A hill in the outskirts of the village,
Resembles a saddled horse;
Foolish men will resemble,
A bad letter written in gold.

This world resembles a river without a bottom,
It will get you drowned, be aware.
Don't be proud of your wealth,
It will come and go in turns.

The one with no brother is powerless,
The one with no son has no wealth.
The one with no wife has no pleasure;
Even good days will resemble grief for him.

The bad brings no benefit,
The one who is good-natured will do no harm,
Riches of this world do not comprise wealth,
Only a son will be your real wealth.

Pepper and salt for a new wound,
Would be like a poison to life.
A mean wife to a good husband,
Resembles an endless slander.

Her bed resembles the one of the snake,
Her embrace resembles one of a dog,
A good wife of a mean husband,
Resembles a cheap jewel.

Magtymguly, hopeless,
Everybody is happy, but I am not.
He who doesn't understand the meaning of words,
Resembles a dog without a tail.

It Will Never Be Equal to a Horse

The work of a donkey is worthless, my friends,
It will never be equal to work done by a horse.
If something could influence an idler,
Please know, there will be no comparison to a delicate man.

Don't believe in the transient world,
Don't be proud of gold and silver,
Don't give your soul to your sons-in-law,
They will be of no comparison to your sibling of the same blood.

If your eyes have seen much,
If you know from each meaning,
The word you said to an ignorant man
Won't compare to a flow of wind.

When you fall ill and are tied to your pillow,
You will have no patience and fortitude.
When you lose your strength and power,
Your sons and daughters will be worse than strangers to you.

Magtymguly says, in good times,
Some laugh, whereas others cry.
Trees providing us with various fruit,
Will become fruitless, of no comparison to Paradise.

He Did Not Suffer When Young

He won't like to work when grown up,
If he did not suffer when young.
After becoming rich he will lose his mind
If he did not have enough in his youth.

An admonition is useless for an ill-natured man,
But for a good-natured one a single word is enough.
For one who has never worn a new robe,
It's easy to take a wrong path.

An armored robe made of steel,
A sharp sword, an Arabian horse,
A young man with no courage,
Will become shameless in battle.

A shepherd won't feel at ease among people,
A crow is careful not to get shot,
A quick-tempered young man won't yield,
When there are too many people.

Put every effort in your service,
Don't spare a piece of bread,
If someone is bleeding, sacrifice your own blood,
For a poor young man who is your guest.

No one will be left in this world,
Wealth never accompanied the soul,
If a young man is not granted a child,
It's as if he has never come to this world.

Silver will look like copper to a diamond,
Even a slave girl will be quite a match for a widower.
A beautiful woman will look quite ugly,
To a young man without a generous nature.

The wealth you've gathered will turn into spiders and mosquitoes,
They'll start sucking your blood,
If you are such a greedy man not willing
To give zakat from your wealth.

Magtymguly won't get lost on his way,
Good words will not affect a bad person,
From the thousands of words you've said, he won't consider at least one,
If God hasn't put it into the heart of a young man.

Soul Is in Inspiration

The Soul is king of the body,
Each word is an inspiration.
On the throne of seven climes,
Each of them has its own function.

The ups and downs of mountains,
The migration of so many people,
The instability of the world,
Is on the will of fate.

Is there one who's been left behind in this world?
It sounds true to me, but false to you,
One white and one black snake,
Are at the service of Suleyman.

Their backs are from emerald stones,
Their forefathers are powerful like camels and their brothers are like rhinos,
With a golden throne and diamond crown,
Courageous beys are his guards.

The months, the epochs will pass by,
The palaces built will grow old,
If the souls meet their beloved ones during the day,
At night they will see them in their dreams.

Three fourths of it is water and oceans,
The remaining fourth is the earth which is full of problems.
Oh, Lord, who knows,
How old this world is?

Magtymguly says support is needed,
Death is an arrow, fate is a bow.
The world is like an unfaithful woman,
Surrounding all of humankind.

See What There Is in It

Let's travel around this world,
And see what there is in it,
The tall buildings built by Iskender and Jamshid.

Its forests are full of lions and tigers,
Grass and flowers, as well as young mountains,
We can also see their dew-damp meadows,
Creeks and springs with mild water flowing down.

The Creator created everything from nothing,
Mountains exist from long ago,
When asked they will tell you about Noah,
We can see ancient games as well.

Rejoice, the transient world, rejoice,
Neither the joyful nor the sad will be left behind,
We can see snow and rain, covering the Milky Way in the sky,
As well as eye-pleasing springs.

Haze round their peaks will not disperse,
It won't turn to fall on to the ground with the time passing,
They will never age, nor die, nor get lost,
We can see the Gorganly Mountains.

Not a single building will remain unseen,
We will see gardens filled with fresh air,
Where lovers once sweetly strolled in,
Where parrots, nightingales had built their nests.

Magtymguly, is there one who will not die?
The angel of death has never been satiated, and the soil never got full,
The sky will never fall down, while the Earth will turn upside down,
The Sun will set and the Moon will appear.

What Would Happen?

Oh, my friends, there is no way to know,
What will happen to us,
Look at this deluding fate,
It will add poison to our food.

The Angel of death will come and open its mouth,
The Earth will embrace the slender waists,
He who came smiling to this world will leave it crying,
It will not take mercy at our tears.

Don't rely on happiness and fate,
It can turn into hundreds of thousands of dreams.
There is no trust in wealth or treasure,
The entire world looks like a dream.

The fate looked at us awry,
It stretches out its hand and bewitches us,
Spreading grain around on the middle of our path,
It laid traps around us.

Magtymguly, if you go to the Hereafter,
You will be asked about your good and bad deeds,
When the precious soul leaves the body,
The soil will be happy to embrace our flesh.

An Indecisive Man

Those in love with their Lord,
The longer you see the more you are disappointed
With an impatient and indecisive man.
A kind-hearted dog is better than
A shameless and unfaithful man.

As years and months go by,
Your fate will turn a hundred directions,
With time passing friends will leave,
An impoverished man left without anything.

A dog will not be reproached by gold,
My words won't influence a fool,
The deeds you wish will not become true,
Because of the man who does not work but only eats.

Everyone wakes up at dawn,
Each has his share from the Lord.
Oh, God, oh, Prophet, the people are
Sick and tired of unreliable men.

Magtymguly spreads around wisdom,
Everyone enjoys the pleasure of his words;
With time passing the soul will be
Disappointed by an indignant shameless man.

The Sultan of Two Worlds

Oh, my friends, Muslims,
The sultan of two worlds,
In ancient times an immortal soul
Of the Prophet was created in a perishable body.

From Moses's Tur Mountains on the Earth,
From a paradise fairy in the heaven,
From the divine radiance of the Messenger,
Moon, Sun, Earth and Sky were created.

Dreaming to see your beautiful face,
I wandered around the mountain of a saint,
Calling and looking for my love,
My soul wandered throughout the world.

I lost my consciousness, taken aback,
When at last I met a brave man,
When I crossed over sixty-six mountains,
And had crossed twelve rivers.

Magtymguly, your soul is not at peace,
What a fire it is you are burning in,
You are separated from everything,
You won't distinguish benefit from harm.

One Will Look for His People

Someone who has been separated from his homeland,
Will moan and groan looking for his people.
Someone who has lost his way,
Will take pains to find it.

In the sky the fate turns round,
On earth the people are in despair;
What a reckless world it is,
Everyone is in search of fortune from the moment he is born.

Someone has a crown of gold,
Someone is a wonderer in need,
Someone is completely poor,
Some look for silk and carpets.

Someone hasn't got bread to eat,
Someone hasn't enough storage for it,
Someone cannot find a robe to put on,
Some people are in search of raw rice to eat.

This world is a high hill,
Some alive and others nearly dead;
Everybody is engaged in something,
Each tries to find his own way.

Time is long but life is too short,
Spring comes first of all four seasons,
The goose flapping its wings in the sky,
Will search for a lake with its eyes.

Magtymguly, you in your sound mind,
Living with tears running down,
Your crazy soul in high spirits,
Will be considering thousands of wishes.

Are Astonished Greatly

Those in love with their Lord,
Are astonished greatly.
Those eyes in search of the beloved,
Are in tears – endless tears.

The Almighty took mercy on him,
A miracle with light and might,
Hoja Ahmet with the dress of a dervish on,
Is in Sayram–Sayram.

Trees growing out of the ground,
Birds with tongues full of prayers,
Dervishes who are in love with Suhan,
Are joyful – in good spirits.

Wake up, my beloved, wake up,
Wander around as a crazy man; be among your people.
Ishmael, a son of Halil,
Is to be sacrificed, in a sacrifice.

Those who stayed in Tur Mountains,
So many saints that turned into angels,
Those who saw your appearance,
Are adhering to the orders of God.

One who enlightened the world,
One who commented on both worlds,
One who explained all the affairs,
All is written in the Quran, the Quran.

Magtymguly, speak out,
Serve Allah for months and years,
The servants who never served,
Will have regrets, huge regrets tomorrow.

Desires of This Transient World

A son of Adam, your thoughts and desires,
Are all desires of this transient world,
If you engage yourself in these thoughts,
They will bring you grief and pain one day.

One day your head will enter the soil,
Your relatives will forget about you,
The prayers you read and the fast you keep will be your mates,
As well as the verses of the Quran on your tongue.

They will attack you from right and left,
Satan will try to block your path,
Strong will and heavy support,
Make up a fortress of the Shariah.

The foundation of this world,
The reason for food, support for the Almighty,
A pillar of the Earth, support for the sky,
Are all supplications made by dervishes.

This life will end, this breath will stop;
Now you can't walk steadily on your feet,
You are the person who was able to tame an elephant,
You will now be eaten by worms.

There are the mountains and stones too,
There are springs and winters too,
There are good and evil deeds,
You will have to confront the challenges sent by fate.

Magtymguly, love is a field,
This field is visited by a soul,
Your soul is a guest in your body,
He who gave life to you will take it back one day.

Will Leave

Oh, a son of Adam, the fate
Will come and cut out your robe.
It will stab you with its dagger,
A killer will spread your blood around.

Do not live with passion for this world,
Wandering in places forgotten by God,
Those whom you visited once
Will pass way at the blink of an eye.

If you die, who will remember you?
The racehorses will stay behind neighing,
The fine young men who rode them,
Will leave and embrace the black soil.

The end of the world is not stable,
Fire is the home of those who forgot their prayers,
Death is a bitter sweetness,
Everyone will taste it and leave this world.

Your soul dreams: I wish I would not die,
I wish not to stay alone in the grave.
If you're disloyal to your Lord,
Faith will run away from you.

Magtymguly, what a world it is,
Looks like a wonderful caravanserai,
The world is like a mean woman,
She will embrace you once and leave.

You Will Be Taken Away

Oh, son of Adam, you will not stay
In this world, you will be taken away.
All your gathered property, halal or haram,
Will remain after your death,

Whatever way you lead in this world,
People will remember only your good and bad words,
Your amazing eyes and flower-like face
Will wither due to the late frosts.

Your blood will leave your body,
Your bones will be left with no work,
Your soul that stayed in you for years,
Will depart you.

Your spring passed, and winter came,
Supplications and fast should be your only worry,
In this world, your head, your sultan,
Who knows what challenges it will encounter?

The souls that come to this world,
Are all like guests to each other,
People of Hoja and Seit tribes, beys and khans,
They all will die in the end.

Devote yourself to the Almighty,
Do not spend your life in vain,
One day you will be taken to a room
With no windows and doors.

Your home will be left in chaos,
Your palaces and caravanserai will be ruined,
The Creator of the Earth and mankind,
Will remain all alone.

Magtymguly is your real servant,
Keep your tongue from saying inappropriate words,
Your right path on the Day of Judgment
Will be the bridge of Syrat.

When Compared with a Good-Natured Man

A mean man not valuing good deeds
Is known only when judged by a good-natured one,
The value of eyes will be known only
When judged by the blind.

It is the distrust of this world
That supports the soul of the crazy one,
The blessing of the healthy ear,
Is known only when judged by the deaf.

Regardless of whether you are a spiritual leader or a young man,
Do not share your secret with others,
A value of a whetstone capable of keeping,
A secret is known only when judged by gold.

The purpose of life in this world is to have
A horse, a wife, and children,
The power of a work camel is
Known only when judged by a thoroughbred camel.

If I am rid from this grief,
If my winter turns into spring,
Magtymguly, my desire,
Is known only when judged by my beloved.

Created Me

Oh, Lord, with your miracle,
You created me from nothing.
By taking me away from my fellow friends,
You made me suffer greatly.

You didn't make me lucky enough,
And didn't hear my supplications.
You didn't make me the father of the world of knowledge,
But made me ever in need of wealth.

By separating me from my relatives and parents,
And from my brother,
By separating me from my people and my land,
You turned me into a wanderer.

Magtymguly, all in grief,
Shedding tears from his eyes,
He makes his pleadings to the Almighty,
You made me suffer so much.

If He Has No Wealth

A fine young man will not have fame,
If he has no wealth or status,
A downcast man will accomplish no work,
If he does not go crazy about it.

If a man has no children,
His name will be forgotten after death,
The spark in the heart won't get ignited,
If there is no intention at the onset.

Weed-eating birds will never hunt,
A man of no trade can't make ends meet;
There is no place in the community,
For the one who has no intelligence.

It is good to move into a new place,
And to fill with carpets a home's most prominent places.
People not fully involved in their lives
Are good only in their graves.

Magtymguly, the one with his head on his shoulders,
Won't feel awkward, neither in battle nor at dinner;
But their meals will be too salty and their enemies will be too strong,
If their friends are not faithful.

In Need of a Beloved

A nice nobleman is in need
Of a beloved worthy of him,
A brave man is in need of an Arab horse,
As well as a diamond saber.

A noble man is a man who is ready to serve his country,
Who is ready to sacrifice his life for his faith;
The brave men are at the service of their motherland,
They all are in need of dignity and courage.

To enjoy themselves for five days,
To lay down the table and share various treats,
To have good fame and honor,
One is in need of wealth.

He who makes a pilgrimage to Mecca, becomes a Haji,
A separation is much more bitter than death,
A smart man needs a saber of faith,
The one in love is in need of his beloved.

Fate will increase your sufferings,
It will deprive you of your will,
Magtymguly, you are in need of your beloved,
The one who has black curls.

Known Only When Far Away

People won't know the value of a good-natured man,
Good-natured men are known only when they are far away.
If God casts a glance onto a person,
Whatever is going to happen is known from the very beginning.

Don't commit sins staying inside your home,
Both your hands and legs will be witnesses against you,
It is a secret to the people, but obvious to God,
A good-natured person is known only when at work.

In this world wealth is your value,
You can do what you aim for;
Everyone will praise you when you are at home,
A brave man is known only when in battle.

If you burn henna you will get a dye,
If you melt gold, you will get a stone,
All horses look the same,
A real horse is known only when in the race.

Hoja, Seit, you influence common people,
And serve as guides to the poor ones,
With nice and smiling faces,
Everyone is known only when in the crowd.

Magtymguly, the day of dreams,
The religion of Islam is good,
The most beautiful girl's beauty
Is known only by her eyes and eyebrows.

A Companion

A good word will please your soul,
If you have a good person as a companion,
If you encounter a bad neighbour,
You will be in search of the way to escape him.

The end of the world is to leave,
The goal here is to accomplish one's deed,
If you become related to an evil man,
Your life will turn into grief.

A single evil word will hurt your heart,
The entire universe dreams of a good man,
He who once has been pleased by someone,
Won't forget and will wish to see him again.

Not everyone is skilled at something,
They have no fear of their enemy,
For a man of charity in this epoch,
There is no place he is worthy of.

Magtymguly will give advice,
Those who understand will remember it,
He who leads evil people,
Will get himself defamed.

Towards the Basin

I've opened my mouth, closed my eyes,
Stretched out my hand towards the basin.
On the basin there was,
A hopeless man ready to be mourned.

The master stood up and invited,
Some were late, others were on time,
The basin was prepared for a hopeless man,
I desired to stop him.

I felt myself immature there,
I suffered because I fell in love,
A red veil covering a flower-like face,
Averted down away from me.

He who wanted to hear of this world,
Will lose all the wealth he had,
Those in love will sacrifice their lives,
If only they were offered a cup.

This world is like a guesthouse,
Those who come will leave this world,
Magtymguly begs for help,
From Hydyr and Ilyas.

Shahs Will Not Abide

Oh, poor man, don't be sad,
The rulers will not abide,
Imposing and magnificent cities,
As well as white buildings won't abide.

If a tongue becomes speechless,
A soul is a diamond, a body is clay,
A nightingale with its thousand songs,
As well as tall mountains won't abide.

I've understood one thing,
The seven continents will collapse
The earth will become twisted,
Mountains will melt and won't abide.

If there is an ordinance from God,
There is no way out and no remedy,
The sky, the Sun and the Moon will shudder,
The stars won't abide as well.

Neither lands nor the countries,
Neither Turks, nor Kurds,
Neither birds, nor wolves,
Creatures with wings won't abide.

Neither dust, nor twister,
Neither courageous, nor staunch,
The elephant, the mosquito and the rhinoceros;
Predators won't abide.

Magtymguly, those ancient rivers,
That witnessed hard times,
And were once abounding in water,
Those rivers won't abide as well.

With Streams

On the top of high mountains,
Clouds will play with rain streams,
Any work which comes with people,
Is a holiday and feast for a brave man.

Those who spoke became deaf and dumb,
Gold, silver corroded and turned into rust,
When a mosquito was equal to an elephant
When they compete with each other.

Calves will run to the pastures,
The good bulls will start first,
The perfect horses will be distinguished,
Even when dressed in old and ragged clothes.

Saints will distance themselves from evil deeds,
The lions from eating leftovers of fox,
Indeed it will make you vomit,
If you find a hair in your food.

A real believer will turn to God,
An evil man will get what he deserves,
Magtymguly, will conceal his faults,
With his treats, saber or words.

Is There Anyone Who Laughed?

Oh, my friends, Muslims,
Is there anyone who laughed but never cried?
Is there anyone who left this transient world,
And then returned back?

Oh, fate, you made some people happy,
You relieved some people from grief,
Some were killed by you,
Is there anyone who is happy with you?

Someone sows seeds of devotion,
Someone suffers a mortal pain,
Some are freed from grief,
Is there anyone who withered without turning yellow first?

I've got to know the joys of this world,
Of its alertness when in grief,
Is there one, who knows the value of health,
Before he gets sick?

This world is of two edges,
One is black; the other one is white,
There are two stations, the distance is far,
Is there anyone who thought about this?

Magtymguly, he who came, will leave
He who settles on this running spring
Will have to move one day;
The candle of youth will get blown down,
Is there any lie in my words?

Pain Will Moan

Oh, my friends, Muslims,
Pain will moan in my heart,
In the hands of a rich man's son,
Playing chess, a mulberry branch will moan.

Don't leave this world as a coward,
You'll lose your mind and die;
A fire will be set on the high mountain,
Dry things will catch fire, but wet ones will moan.

I've seen a maiden among Turkmen moving somewhere,
The smell of musk is coming from her hair,
On the meadows, among the herd,
The foals of wild mustangs will moan.

Magtymguly, my words are true,
But still there is no one who believes the words of truth,
If a noble young man has no son,
His hearth will disappear, his people will moan.

If a Garden Has No Pomegranates

What does a gardener need a garden for,
If there are no pomegranates on its trees?
Let a son not be born to a father,
If he has no self-respect and dignity.

A jungle won't be a garden for a nightingale,
A hill won't be a mountain for a mountain goat,
A racehorse won't be better than any other horse,
If it does not have good manners.

If one drinks sherbet, it will taste like honey,
His every day will turn into a year,
Her flower-like skin will turn pale as the color of ashes,
If a beauty does not have a beloved.

Magtymguly, they will say secretly,
Those who love should be called beloved,
If a young man does not have sweet words,
He is called an animal.

Today Is His Time

Tell a young man, who has no shame or dignity,
Today is his time.
Let him gather riches like Karun,
The treasury is empty–it is his time.

Oh, what should I do, my luck is wretched,
My heart and my soul are torn into pieces,
Tell my wishes to my beloved,
That she is a remedy for my suffering.

My joyful market fell apart,
My pain is increasing day by day,
My eyes are not able to see anymore,
As if there is a haze of the mountains in front of them.

Having seen your face—the only child,
I came walking from Khiva,
I came riding my horse through the desert,
I came; this is the order from God.

Magtymguly, your pain is obvious,
You properly explained everything,
But learned to hold your tongue, not to get into trouble,
Your eloquence is awesome.

Ruined It

Look, how my fate has ruined the building of my poor soul.
Look at what the world ruined,
Creating the pain in my heart,
Having deprived me of my dignity.

If only prosperity comes from God,
If only sad eyes start shining with happiness,
If only the poor realize the value of the motherland,
These are the things that we have been missing.

Let a brave man be your brother,
Otherwise you will not save your head from trouble.
Your devoted friend will look for your demerits,
And will try to spread them among your people.

What a brave man without a horse,
No wolves will be found near him if he has one.
Countries with gardens and palaces
All have turned into plain fields.

Magtymguly, now lost his mind,
Will an old man say his words before leaving this world?
Lions who roamed at dawn early
In the morning came wondering.

Will Never Be Brave

A hero will be born to a brave man,
A coward will never be brave, indeed.
There is a fire burning in a wolf's eyes
Jackals and foxes will never be wolves, indeed.

Speak aloud what you know,
If a nightingale is separated from a rose,
Know this, a son of Adam, there is no other land,
Other than your Motherland.

If this world is wonderful,
If the whole world is full of sun rays and sunshine,
If God took mercy on you in the first place,
Neither body nor soul will be suffering from pain.

Magtymguly, perceive it with all your brain,
You poured so many tears from your eyes,
Your head of grief has reached the age of fifty,
There is no pain worse than that.

Brought Trouble onto Us

Our brave men passed away,
Fate brought trouble onto us.
Children being taken away from fathers;
Fate brought trouble onto us.

This transient world has turned into fire,
There is no intention of an uncertain soul,
Not a single one was left safe,
Fate brought trouble onto us.

Karun was deprived from his intention,
Look, Nuh was deprived of his arch,
A nightingale was separated from its flower,
Fate brought trouble onto us.

The Death subjects our temporary lives to challenges,
Magtymguly, is trampled down,
On the surface of this world,
Fate brought trouble onto us.

Will Not Awaken

Oh, my friends, my failed fate,
Won't awaken days and nights,
Neither my tree that lost its fruit,
Nor my spring will awaken.

Oh, friends, Muslim brothers,
Nor women who left this world in a pure state,
With their souls dumped into mud,
Nor will the geese of my lakes awaken.

The garden flowers have withered,
Now the wind of the Hazar will not blow,
That Arabic has become bitter,
And the Indian melody will not awaken.

My peers and dear friends,
My fate has torn my liver into two equal pieces,
Magtymguly, this transient world,
Will drink and eat, but won't kill its thirst for souls.

With Brave Men

Real men will never regret,
If they fight with brave men,
A separation ruined my fortune,
with my nation, with my land.

Fate will pick the newly blossomed flowers,
It will make a nightingale impatient,
If a mudflow doesn't flow along the cliff,
A rock will start crying badly.

No one could escape from death,
It won't be taken by a courageous man as a companion,
Lions will not be hurt,
By a hundred thousand jackals and wolves.

My destiny made me a prisoner,
The dam of my fate has collapsed,
My love has gone, my happiness is lost,
Magtymguly, all due to misery.

Until He Knows What It Means

An ignorant person will laugh at the wise word,
Until he knows what it means.
The top of the mountain will be covered with fog,
Until the wind blows from the Hazar.

A wise man won't drink wine,
No one will abandon a good nation,
The Creator won't forgive his sinful one,
Until he shows his devotion to the Quran.

A Sufi will speak his word of wisdom,
A wretched coward will care for his own sin,
A camel will cry going out into the desert,
Until she finds her baby colt.

The snow will remain on the mountain,
A coward won't do people's work,
A brave fellow won't stop worrying,
Until he marries a beauty of his heart.

An old man will consider his time,
An infidel will be grief-stricken,
Courageous men will always cry,
Until they find a true brave companion.

The life boat will sink into mud,
Its suffering will grow day by day,
A vindictive young man will keep his grievance,
Until he has had his revenge.

No one will stay in this world forever,
Fate won't be our companion.
A young child won't be appreciated
Until he plays and laughs for a while.

Everyone wants to marry a beauty,
But her choice depends on God's will.
A brave man is impatient,
Until he embraces his beloved.

How many evils will be seen?
How many good or bad words will be spoken?
The hunters will keep going to the mountains,
Until they become very old.

My name became famous,
It will go from one tongue to another,
Magtymguly, land onto a flower,
Until it drops and withers due to the cold.

Keep Me Safe

Our beys will gather for a council,
Ignorant fate, keep me safe,
You inflict trouble on everyone;
Ignorant fate, keep me safe.

The bird of prosperity flew up to the sky,
God granted his blessing, cast a glance,
The Moon and the Sun both got ashamed on seeing this;
Ignorant fate, keep me safe.

The advice of the wise men is followed,
The fate is sent to eternity,
Staying ignorant in prison;
Ignorant fate, keep me safe.

You inflicted so much grief and pain,
You took the souls given temporarily,
You put us through a lot of troublesome time;
Ignorant fate, keep me safe.

Cowards became lions,
All women turned into leopards,
My people turned into bears;
Ignorant fate, keep me safe.

I suffered so much pain,
I never tasted the joys of life,
I held the hand of a beauty not seen before;
Ignorant fate, keep me safe.

Magtymguly says, oh God,
The end of the world has gotten closer,
The top of the mountain is covered by the mist of separation;
Ignorant fate, keep me safe.

Indeed

Oh, my friends, a human being,
Was created from soil, indeed,
A human, originally made of soil,
Is to get mixed with soil again, indeed.

Some in trouble and in worry,
Some in sadness and in sorrow.
It was described in a sacred verse,
Death and Resurrection are both true, indeed.

For your guilt you're in trouble,
In sorrow, in worry, in need,
It is true that one will be questioned
In the darkness of the grave, indeed.

When the angel of death comes after you,
This state will disappear in your eyes,
If Dedjal comes with a great passion,
It is true that the Sun and the Moon tell us the time, indeed.

When the Shariah laws are not followed anymore,
When the world is covered with dark ignorance,
When the deadline of promises gets closer,
It is true that the End of the World has come, indeed.

Infidels turn into a great sorrow,
The Prophet reaches the presence of God,
Israfyl prepares his scales,
It is true that all of your sins and good deeds are to be weighed, indeed.

That day will turn into panic and darkness,
The scale of the skies appears on Judgment Day,
The Great Provider of all our necessities will gather the Council,
It is true that the Prophet will show his mercy, indeed.

Some cross the Syrat bridge like birds,
Some cross it in a thousand years,
Sinful servants will burn and turn into ashes,
It is true that they will go to the Hell, indeed.

The thirsty ones will be given poison,
The hungry ones will be given zakgun,
Scorpions will be poured upon them,
It is true they are to be bitten by snakes and spiders, indeed.

Those who stay there will cry,
The hell fire will burn them all,
Becoming weak when burning in the fire,
Their voices will be heard in the skies, indeed.

Magtymguly, you'll say I've taken it,
If you take from someone forcefully,
There's no other way, you have to return it,
What you took, you must return, indeed.

When Gathered

The more slaps the world is given the more turbulent it will become.
When will the soul become relaxed and gathered together?
Be engaged in the work needed in the hereafter, distance yourself from the rest;
Was there anyone who could keep this world? It shall pass away, turning to mud.

Where is Benijan who used to cut mountains with his nails,
And Suleyman whose orders were adhered to by water and wind,
Where is Iskender, the brave wrestler Rustem,
In whose name are you going to rule the world?

We're tired of this day's merciless life,
With too much time, no hindering — just a useless day,
In childhood, in youth, your day goes happily;
In your old age it makes you fall into deep grief.

It is common knowledge, that those who come will leave.
Those who know what they got themselves involved in, know what is needed where they go.
Those ignorant ones who relaxed in sleep with no concerns,
What a disaster, they went with their hands empty, with demerits.

Could you find the courageous truth,
Then use its dust as stibium for your eyes?
The grief of your sin as deep as the waters of the Red Sea,
Dried out by a real penance, being a true remedy of it.

First you should set your good intention,
Search for hopes in every corner,
Using your knowledge, always say good words,
If you do not find good words, then sit, not uttering a word.

Magtymguly, don't forget the name of Allah,
Be patient when you confront bad and be thankful when good is happening,
Visit a cemetery and think about it,
There are so many people of glory mixed in with the soil.

The Best of Months

Twenty four hours in twelve months,
The best of months is called the month of Ramadan,
During the time of protection, on the earth,
The best of the houses is the one highly respected and glorious.

Oh, Creator, your miracles are endless,
Your wonders are awesome,
Oh Lord, it is a secret not easy to understand,
You put the best of waters into darkness.

A crow does not belong among tall trees,
When the songs of nightingales sing among the flowers,
Behind the earth, in wealthy mountains,
The best of the caves is the one taken by the dragon.

If you find time and plead to God,
Your mind will be astonished to see such insanity.
Your heart will be broken; your body will be in pain,
If the jackal gets the best of the hunt.

Passion has burned me down, my soul is ill;
My sufferings are too much; failure is my only fate.
This is a tradition coming from ancient times,
A hedgehog usually gets the best melon.

If you know the language of a predator, it will become your friend,
Don't take the true deeds of your neighbor as misdeeds,
If you are smart enough, try to hide the misdeeds,
And spread the good deeds of a noble man.

Magtymguly, this is the time when
Good-natured people cry and meet ill-natured persons,
Like the brothers of Joseph who thought,
He was not worthy of the best of places.

Its Value is Known by a Horse

A donkey does not feel inferior to a horse,
One can see its value only by a horse,
But when we say a horse, we do not imply that all horses are equal,
True horses are known in the field they belong to.

In your childhood, you did not know you were a powerful bey,
An evil person won't take your advice or listen to your word,
If you are wise, never ask the origin of a young man,
He will demonstrate it through his manners and deeds.

Your hungry eyes will never have enough in this world,
Not every lion can become a tiger,
When we say a young man, we know that all young men are not equal,
The true young men will be known when welcoming their guests.

If wealth comes to the one to become rich,
He will be in need of support and people around,
A young brave man will show who he is through his deeds,
He can be distinguished in battle and conversation.

Magtymguly, the tears of the poor people,
Will burn down the mountains, burn the stones,
The misdeeds of the cruel inflicting sufferings upon the poor,
Will be obvious on the Day of Judgment.

Inspiration Will Be Ignited

The time will come when an idea will flash through my head,
A dream will strike, and ignite my inspiration.
If my heart is inspired, then my mind is clear,
Thoughts will keep me busy, grief will hinder my memory.

If a dervish starts moaning at dawn,
Takes a rope from his waist to put around his neck,
If someone, loved by God, prays with bad intentions,
Fate will shudder, and the skies will burn.

A fool will consider himself a match to the clever one;
He will commence some work, and only afterward think about it.
He will fetter your aptitude, and abate your wisdom,
He will make all your experience in vain by not following your advice.

The creator cherished such zealots as Ali,
Respecting elders is an ancient tradition.
People of seventy two nationalities bury their dead;
Dog worshippers burn the bodies of their dead.

Magtymguly, if a bowl is granted by God,
And it overflows, bringing your dreams,
If lovers moan from their hearts,
It will shatter mountains and burn stones.

If Seized

There are so many deeds in this world, the bad ones,
He who is seized with rage for nothing, does nothing worth anything,
He who is in love, and is far away, separated by a long distance from his beloved,
Feels that each day is the end of the world for him.

Do not linger with your friend, or he will lose his profit,
Do not linger with your enemy, or he will learn your secret,
Do not try to recover your loan from the poor, and do not be indebted to the rich;
Any work is hard for someone who does not get it.

Would the soil be ready to swallow you so soon,
Would the wisdom lie there in the soil with no sorrow,
Would any disgrace be worse than this,
If one leaves this world with no fame, or comes with nothing.

If you had a house with ten floors and iron walls,
Death still will find you if that is God's order.
The true man will never turn away from danger,
If this trouble is ordered by God.

They will pretend they're Sufis and boast,
Verify their words with those who know for sure,
A sincere tear shed at one day's dawn is better
than a hypocrite's hundred years spent worshipping God.

The rich, locking the door of generosity,
Increase the number of spiders and snakes in hell.
Look at Sufis of this era and time
They won't be selective and eat whatever is served.

Magtymguly, speak up about whatever you consider right,
Instead of wasting your life, earn for your afterlife,
For a good man who marries a wicked woman
Every day will turn into hell until he dies.

Humankind

Whether asleep or awake, he will always keep in his mind,
Whatever work is chosen by humankind,
The grief of being poor won't make you depressed,
If a man becomes a beggar wishing to have a wife.

He who is not afraid to commit a sin will be in disgrace,
It will become known on Judgment Day,
If a human being agrees with his destiny,
He is the sultan, the king within his worldly estate.

The deeds of the lucky man will be seen beforehand,
If the entire world fits in one hand, it will appear to be strange.
All the deeds done in one's youth will seem strange,
For a human becomes smarter after forty.

Everyone who did not understand the meaning of a word,
He who cannot find any remedy to the illness he has got,
On Judgment Day will regret all the demands he had made,
If a human being is happy with what God grants him.

Think of the paths of the world and its state;
Do not take for granted the state of the world,
Magtymguly, one will love his work,
If a human being can become younger after forty.

From the Unfaithful

Don't give your heart to the unfaithful,
Look, who has seen loyalty from unfaithful people?
Don't put yourself into many sufferings for nothing;
Who has benefited from such pains?

Listen to the melody of love from a distance,
If you're afraid of pain, don't go there from the very start,
If you're short of remedies for a sickness called love,
Go and ask those who have encountered such a disaster.

My word is advice, be ready to listen.
I'm a servant of a slave, who is in need of such a word,
You should know that a woman, flirting with forty men, is better
Than those who speak too much and look for trouble.

He who gets a bowl of pure drink,
Will brighten his soul like a mirror,
The world is a seven-headed creature swallowing everything,
Even those who run away won't escape these troubles.

Magtymguly, don't sleep satisfied with what you have,
You will be sleeping long in your grave-clothes,
Having left his master, can one find,
What he needs, asking poor slaves for it!

For the Moon and Sun to Set

Sufis of sixty or seventy years old,
Little time is left for your moon and sun to set.
Foxes not seeing a hound in the deserts and valleys
Will wish to kill a sleeping lion.

A crow will say, "There is no falcon like me,"
If thousands of crows gathered together they won't be worthy of a single hawk,
A yellow lizard which curses the Sun,
Is getting ready to swallow a dragon.

A single mountain deer won't let a hundred badgers hunt it.
A single lion's cub won't let ninety foxes catch it.
A dead snake won't let a hundred lizards swallow itself
Will our brain be capable of understanding these things?

Even at seventy they won't forget repentance,
They will flirt joyfully with unfaithful women,
If infidels destroy the Kaaba with revenge,
A disbeliever will go and sell its logs.

Just have a look at this epoch, the turning world,
Their objective is just to torture the poor,
Even a dervish following the path of God,
Isn't given a chance to rest.

My heart knows no tolerance, no patience.
It's an evil thing for a man to mistrust a man;
Being tired of this world,
I am ready to abandon it for good.

Magtymguly says, now I know my luck is wretched;
My rumors are strong; my destiny is a failure.
My intention is Kaaba and my wish is to go on a pilgrimage,
I have zeal to fulfill my obligation for a pilgrimage.

Not Worthy of His Dream

So many people's fate is in poverty,
It is not worthy of a good dream you see in sleep.
So many people suffer to find a piece of hard bread,
But they will never try this tasty treat.

For those who ask, I could say I have fire in my body.
There are so many words worth more than a hundred tumen.
Springs without rain, plants and grass
Are not worthy of a winter passed with joy.

There are smart men, who wear felt headwear,
They will provide you the meaning if you urge them for it,
Many fools that are wearing fancy clothes,
Are not worthy of a turban, tied around their head.

If you say words of prayer to someone who has no idea,
Even if you put the Prophet's hadis in front of them,
Even if you put thousands of words into their head,
These words wouldn't even touch the outer parts of their ears.

If children hurt their parents,
God will not forgive them until they repent,
When the time comes, they will not know what to be engaged with,
No one is capable of being good at every job.

So many people will not find wealth, thus be poor,
So many people will be overwhelmed by their richness in this world,
So many people will be worth nothing in their youth,
So many people will not be worthy of the years they lived.

Magtymguly, praying is my real devotion,
My soul is confused; I have committed a lot of mistakes.
There are men that are worth more than the thousand tumen you gave them,
There are people who are not worthy of the food they are treated to.

If There Is No Salt Either

If you are treated to ninety different dishes,
And if there is neither taste nor salt in any of them,
You are not aware what lies ahead of you,
And it is a challenge if there are no eyes on your head.

You have feet to walk, and hands to take,
But is there anyone who is thankful for his health,
You have ears to know that you hear,
Who will be there to correct, if you have no words on your tongue?

You gave life out of nothing and provided,
Faith will grow in the garden of the soul.
If you are a human being, then know your Master,
Even if your Master never encountered you face to face.

He who believes in his destiny will never lessen his wealth,
Will never hide his words among those who know words.
The soul won't get inspired and the tongue won't speak,
If there is no fire of love in every heart.

Year by year there will be an increase of shortages,
If God himself does not take care of providing.
The word of the world will seem like a treat with no salt,
If there is no mention of ladies in your talk.

Close your eyes, and live your life with your teeth clenched.
When you live up to the season of spring, do not forget your winter,
Always take the risk, leaving your success to God,
You will accomplish your work, though not quickly, if you are patient.

Magtymguly, I am wandering in my dreams,
I imagine many attractive things.
Those who hear my words, hopefully, will not be ashamed,
If my words are not deep in meaning compared to those of my people.

Will Throw Stones upon You

If you talk for an hour with a fool,
Beware, he might not be able to keep your secret,
If you become friends with a faithless beloved one,
You will lose all your teeth because of grief.

A fool will not be able to stand a prosperous life for five days,
A lizard will not be able to swallow the dead dragon.
Remember, the friendship with a bear will not last long,
If it gets angry, it will throw stones upon your head.

A shepherd of a donkey won't recognize a horse,
A generous one will be recognized among his people, but a just one will be recognized in a council,
A horse will be recognized by the field, whereas respect will be valued by a guest,
A son of a generous man will treat you generously.

A young man's goal is to have a beloved, a sword and a horse,
A cowardly man will bring disgrace to his people,
If an evil-natured man finds a fight in his village,
He will throw endless fists upon a brave son's head.

Magtymguly says that the leader of the young men
Will have many devoted friends in the gathering,
The wives of the young men in battle
Will put their heads with dignity on the battlefield.

There Won't Be a Time

He who comes across my prayer will grow like a flower,
There is no better time than the season of flowers,
The fire of my anger is capable of turning everything into ashes,
One won't find any blossoming garden among those ashes.

A soul is temporary; the dead body is in its eternal home;
My soul is looking for inspiration; my heart is in pain;
My thoughts are of maturity, my eyes are looking for bravery;
Because of my severe terms not a single brave man is found.

Serve the gracious Allah with all your heart,
Don't be misled by wealth and gambling.
A human is a guest in the house of the world,
One day will come, that guest won't be found in this house.

Don't slumber in the dark of the night, wake up
Whatever you give, give it yourself
Prepare for death when you're alive
One day will come; this soul won't be found in this body.

Wherever I go to please my soul,
It finds only strife, hostility and wrangling,
Sermons are not preached, the Quran is not read,
No good manners or tact to please the soul are found.

I have a lot of supplications, my complaints and moans are endless;
My fate is hopeless, my body is weak.
I hide from gatherings, desire only loneliness,
But I cannot find a place where I can be in peace.

Magtymguly, the soul has given fate its body;
If one can resist temptation it is a deed of praise.
Oh, what a dreadful thing it is not to understand the pain,
No remedy will be found for the pain of youth.

You Will Break Stones

When your fate wakes up and wealth becomes your companion,
If you bit into a mountain, you would break stones;
If your fate goes wrong and your luck becomes miserable,
Even thin porridge will break your teeth.

If you enter the ocean fearing your death,
What is the benefit of fear for the soul which is going to pass away?
If your life came to an end, your bowl of life is full,
Even the straw of the poppy will break your head.

Listen to all the words of knowledgeable men,
In the far end your falsehood will get you nowhere,
Words of gratitude for good deeds will add years to your life,
A curse will ruin you, and shorten your life.

The soul will be happy for the wise man's words,
The talent will be ashamed with the work of the fool,
A coward will boast himself a smart person in a big gathering,
But when confronted he will drive anyone mad.

Magtymguly, do not ask for advice from an unintelligent man
Who wandered around in the deserts.
Though he has lived a long life, if you give him a full bowl in a small gathering,
He won't be able to eat the meal, and break the dish instead.

This Is the Time When

My friends, do not be in deep sleep at dawn,
This is the time when the doors are open for wishes,
And saintly men are granted blessings,
This the time when God shares his light.

Do not be sinful or you will burn down,
Know yourself and stay away from vanity,
This is the right time to repent, come back to your senses,
This is the time when sins are forgiven.

May God protect you from the fire of separation,
Do not get lost on the right path of all travelers,
Beware, this is the time when bowls of love
Are being drunk from the hands of a friend.

Even though you live a hundred years in this world,
A day will come when your body will turn into the soil,
This is the time when you can be freed from your vanity,
Gathering on the field of denial.

Magtymguly, you are all in thoughts of this world,
When young you gave your soul to gambling,
Now, when you stepped into the house of thirty,
This is the time when tears must be shed.

Showing off Their Clothes

Oh Muslims, the source of the materialistic world
Is in the habit of showing off clothes to each other,
Whimsicalities are peculiar to young men, whereas girls are coquettish,
And wrestlers are in search of a fighting field.

Death has put its arrow into its bow,
One never knows when one will penetrate your soul.
Having chosen involvement in the fight,
Your life won't be able to last long.

You are surrounded by an iron trap,
The lion of death is lying there in expectation.
Whereas you are sleeping soundly in peace,
Your bad fate is waiting with its sword in its hand.

Not being ashamed of the Lord, having reached the age when your beard is gray,
The tongue is never tired of gossiping, nor are your teeth from eating haram.
If you are involved in good deeds, do things you think you are worthy of in shelter,
Don't be lazy, lying there moaning and groaning.

Everyone will have to see that last breath of reckoning,
There is no way of escaping the death ordered by the Lord,
Magtymguly, there will be no shortcomings at all,
If a man confronts his death having embraced his belief.

This Deed

Oh, man, don't show courage for a bad deed.
A day will come when they will put this deed of yours in front of you,
Do not adhere to greed; do not follow Satan's path;
Know, a day will come he will be judging you for this deed.

Your greed will say: "Bit him up, what a pleasure!"
Your soul will say: "Oh, no, stop, the Lord is there!"
You might not see him, but he is keeping his eye on you,
So please, be ashamed, be afraid to continue this deed.

One road leads you to a sin, the other to a blessing.
You will be asked to give an answer on the Day of Judgment,
He who has good deeds will be appreciated; whereas the wrongful one will be tortured.
There is no doubt, remember, always remember this deed.

Your life is a one-hour spring passing by,
What will happen if you saw God during this spring?
Good deeds will bring about happiness, whereas misdeeds will bring only shame,
Don't take responsibility for this deed.
Do not keep your head up to the sky and your chest to the wind,
Do not let your soul get frightened a bit,
Do not utter a word which is not yet in your heart,
Let the ear of your will hear about this deed.

You are a temporary guest in this world; you will firmly perform deeds,
How long will you stay in this world?
Whatever you do in this world you will have to make an answer for,
Your deeds and wrongdoings will all be counted.

Satan will say: "What a joyful deed, do it with no hesitation!"
The Merciful will say: "Put an end to this intention for greed."
Magtymguly says: "Get up and put your hands on the burning coals;
If you can tolerate that, then go, do this deed."

Just by Looking at My Appearance

Not asking frankly to understand my sufferings,
How can he judge just by looking at my appearance?
Not becoming of mature age to be able to twist the ear of my soul,
I won't be able to tell what sufferings I have gone through.

I don't understand what my end will look like,
I have stayed away from ill-natured men for so long,
Seventy seven times I am grateful to the Creator,
Whether bad or good, whatever there is for me to confront.

Oh, dear, looking frankly into our eyes,
Do not show disbelief in the words by considering them not true,
Bread earned fairly will brighten the eyes,
Know this when you are deprived of my bread and food.

You must be happy with oat bread if you can find it,
If there is no value for life, forget your hope—
You will hear your soul utter, "Oh, Lord," and lifting up toward the skies,
It will desire to free itself from the footwear, the soft leather boots and the turban.

Magtymguly, bearing the humiliation of the enemies,
I used to suppress my anger.
Having spent the spring of my childhood,
There is no way to avoid the winter of old age.

Do Not Trust In the Hands of Fate

Fate was cunning with the entire world;
Do not trust my will into the hands of fate.
If the bird of my soul flies in whatever direction,
Don't deprive it of wings, tail or feathers.

He who has no wealth is gullible, but the one who has all always complains.
If seven men are ignorant, one is willing.
Rich men like to talk nonsense, old people like to boast.
You cannot get rid of the gray within the barrel of white paint, once it gets there.

It is not an easy thing for a man to be the leader of a horde,
One wearing silk and silver will attract the attention of many girls and boys,
An elderly woman will look gracious to a widower's eyes,
He will look around noticing even the blind and lame.

The wheel of fortune turned to its left,
All human beings, coming to this world, confront endless suffering,
Seventy two nations being all apart,
Don't dare to take one part to add to the other.

If I die on the road and if they throw me there,
I do not mind being walked over,
If they remember me and say: "Magtymguly,"
The eyes will cause cracks on the ears that have heard of me.

Engaged in Trifles

Oh, an ignorant man, you are occupied by your sufferings,
You have spent your life engaged in trifles,
The world is a snake; you lean on it, and sleeping,
How can one be at ease lying with a snake?

Earn your faith, don't be so ignorant,
Do not deliberately throw yourself into the fire,
So, spend your life awake, do not sleep,
You will be in the grave after so much suffering.

Whatever direction you chose, it will take you to the grave.
If you earn good deeds, your grave will be lighted,
If you have a good nature, you will be granted a place in Paradise; fairies will be at your service,
If you are ill-natured, you'll be burned with fire.

The moment your eyes are closed, you will be separated from all your wealth,
After your death those who stayed alive won't know your state,
Whatever deed you have been engaged in, evil or good,
You will always confront them as if they accompany you forever.

Originally infidels won't get mixed with Muslims,
A true Muslim won't ever commit a haram deed,
He who chooses a blind man to guide him on his trip,
Won't cover any distance, nor will arrive anywhere.

With Embers

I have no one to ask to pass my wishes to my beloved,
I am burned down with embers of the fire of love,
Let her come and extinguish the fire with her own hands,
Otherwise, it won't get extinguished, neither with heavy rain nor ice.

Those who came passed, and left room for those to come in the future,
A coward repealed friendship, but a brave one retained it.
My beloved added more pain to my wound,
Sprinkling salt and pepper on to it.

I won't find my beloved, but if found, she won't lend her hand;
My destiny won't wake up and happiness won't smile.
Neither my heart will get relaxed, nor will my soul get satisfied,
Until my eyes see the face of my friend.

No one will know what pain and suffering I am going through,
Neither Jesus nor Lukman will find a remedy for that.
He who comes to this world won't stay; the haze won't leave the head.
Each time I confront a challenge due to my word.

With much love you will collect the riches of the world,
Striving for a coin, you will hurt the feelings of hundreds.
A world is a river, a body is a raft, and you will turn over,
How long you'll be along these steppes.

Is there anyone who could
Take at least one piece of wealth with him?
First you all are in grief and in the end everything is ruined,
You'll get mixed with dust and soil too.

Magtymguly, what is the place you will stay in?
Whose world is it where you are engaged in hard work?
By fate, you'll go to a grave one span long,
If God is willing, you will receive grave-clothes six arshin long.

The Soul Never Dies

The tongue is alive thanks to the order of the Lord,
Though the eyes are closed, the soul never dies.
Belief is a new flower in the garden of the soul,
Once blossomed, it will never fade away.

The state of health is better than any treat,
The blessing of God is better than any service,
If the fate of death comes directly after you,
Pleading a thousand times won't keep your soul.

Young men, listen to my words,
Put an end to your hopes of world friendship,
Whatever part of love and desire is bigger,
It won't leave you at peace days and nights.

Oh, son of Adam, you are born to leave this world,
You realize there is a place for you to sleep,
You will try your best to have your own world.
But probably, you aren't smart enough to realize this dream.

Hey, a man of high dignity enjoying the world's wealth,
I'm a poor man, I can't speak a lot,
This market is where the world's fate is such a skilfull gambler,
That a human being is not capable of winning it.

The body is satisfied with food and drink,
Wheareas a sweet word is surprisingly pleasant to the ears of the soul,
The soul will have no good advice,
Likewise water reaching the rocky stone, it won't do any good.

Magtymguly, youthful time is like spring,
For healthy people it looks like a pleasant talk and music,
Joyful days will seem not enough, though lasting for a hundred years.
Whereas bad days will never come to end, though not many.

Oh, It Will Be Blocked

If God is willing, I shall go on a long journey.
Oh, without his blessing, the path I am to take will be blocked,
I'll go out unto the deserts as a bewildered Mejnun,
There I'll definitely choose you, mountains, to be my place of settlement.

I've passed the days of youth in joy and fun,
And thus reached the period of maturity,
My soul started shaking with the sufferings of this world,
My entire body got overwhelmed with mountains, one higher than the other.

Distancing myself from the thoughts about my childhood,
I've approached the edge of maturity.
My head stuck in mud, there is no way out,
Oh, I remember the times that have passed.

He who had a desire to try all four directions,
Not being aware, engaging in evil deeds,
Becoming weak when getting old,
Oh, he will be regretting and shedding tears.

Those who learned their lesson from the words of Magtymguly,
Will fall into deep thought and tears will start flowing from their eyes,
All things will find change by themselves,
Oh, my God, why are these mountains not falling?

It Is Stubborn, My Friends

Oh, dervishes, true believers, prosperous rich men,
The fate's turn is stubborn, my friends
Praying in reproach will not be counted,
Don't rely on wealth; it is all in vain, my friends.

If noses become skinny, faces turn yellow,
Lips get dry, tongues become speechless,
Nails turn purple and eyes become dull,
Everything except faith is nothing, my friends.

Your foundation is a handful of soil; your breath is a single sniff,
Come to your senses, your work is useless,
A body is a temporary place of shelter for the soul with not enough air to breathe,
A soul is a blindfolded bird, my friends.

Do not be ignorant; whoever comes to this world will leave one day,
Don't spend your life in joy and fun in this world, there are worse things.
The caravans will be set forth; will walk keeping the line,
It is a never ending move, my friends.

The angel of death will come one day and make you frustrated,
Those who leave, won't return, this is the way,
Distances are far, loads are heavy
Start up early, or it's going to be late, my friends.

You'll be saved if you die on the path of God,
You'll satisfy him if you give the best of robes,
It'll become your shelter if you give bread to the needy,
It's indeed equal to a pilgrimage to provide a hungry man with bread, my friends.

What we consider this world is made of just two pieces,
One of them is black, the other is white,
A dream you have one night is not there the following day,
A dream is a sample of this world, my friends.

Magtymguly, obey this order,
Don't lose yourself being occupied with wealth,
Stuff of a hundred years for five days' life
Just think, what a world, my friends.

Buried, My Friends

Lukman Hekim who lived forty four hundred years
Had his head buried in the black soil, my friends,
The angel of death grasped Rustem's reins,
Who had a strong racing horse and was armed heavily, my friends.

Joseph's strong desire is with Jacob,
His love is in his heart, pain is in his body,
Is there anyone favored by this cruel fate?
Even Joseph was sold into slavery, my friends.

Sultan Iskender who ruled the universe,
Couldn't find a remedy from death,
Solomon whose throne was carried by the wind,
Didn't remain and left this world as well, my friends.

None of the three hundred and thirteen prophets remained,
Where is the vizier of Asaf-Suleyman?
Where is that just prophet, a lion of God?
The black soil has swallowed them all, my friends.

Magtymguly will say, don't sit there in ignorance,
Do not make your fragile soul suffer long,
Don't live this life in grief,
It is a short period, it has gone, my friends.

It Won't Descend from the Sky, My Friends

The soul, not being at ease, rose from its seat.
It flew up and won't descend from the sky, my friends.
It has an intention which occupies its mind,
Indeed, it won't give up this intention, my friends.

It has tasted the sugar of love,
Now it won't listen to the advice given by clerics,
Rose from its venue, went across the dam,
It will never be back to occupy its place, my friends.

Having considered love wisely and consciously,
Can one who is in love and inspired by it come to his senses?
Those who tasted pure wine from the hands of their beloved,
Once they taste it, won't be satiated, my friends.

There is a script in the hair of Fatima,
It will be read when people are chosen for the Hereafter,
There is such a fire in the hearts of lovers,
Indeed, it doesn't burn as these fires do, my friends.

Magtymguly, love will get inspired on its own,
Love is known to make friends strangers to each other, my friends,
It will burn one down without fire, and flare up with no wind,
Once ignited it will never get extinguished, my friends.

Be a Slave

Instead of being a bey of worthless people,
It's better to be a slave of someone prosperous,
Instead of being at the service of an ill-natured bey,
It's better to turn into ashes in the shade of a real bey.

Quit evil deeds, focus on good ones,
A griffon will also say, "my nestling is cute."
Curses will decrease the breed of wolves;
Like sheep, be on friendly terms with those on all four sides of you.

If you are Solomon just listen to an ant,
Listen to its words, get its answers,
If you are a governor, warm up your nation like the Sun,
Be water in a ditch and wind in a wind-current.

What a deed—to satisfy one's greed not doing anything,
It's foolish to boast about yourself as a good man,
If you want to be successful in each bazaar,
Become money in the pockets of good men.

Magtymguly, each breath of yours is counted,
Sooner or later each man will get what's prepared by his fate,
Stop boasting if you are a human being,
Be the pride of all the people—good or bad.

Turned Out to Be Sandy

Oh, Allah, what a phenomenon is this?
What I thought to be a pure drink, turned out to contain sand,
What a bad, ungodly, unlucky fate it is,
Whatever I eat as halal turns out to be bad.

No one will know my secret even if he kills himself,
If poor people get to know, it's thanks to God,
Happiness, joyful life to enjoy,
The one who is my companion turns out to be very sad.

I'm used to being distressed and to be in grief,
I've nobody to talk to and share my problems with,
I went to a side of the village asking for a house,
Whoever I met there was either numb or speechless.

Whoever I stretch out my hands to would complain about me,
Whoever I share my secret with would spread it easily around,
Those whom I consider poor and take mercy on,
Turned out to be stronger than a giant.

Magtymguly, whatever I've seen is hard to count,
Those to whom I stretched out my hands in hope,
Those whose village I visited, hoping for a brave man indeed,
Turned out to be ...

If He Doesn't Have What He Has to Own

This is the epoch we have—they'll be unnoticed,
If young a man doesn't have what he has to own.
His words worth a hundred tumen won't be taken for a coin,
If a person has no trust.

The body is a stifling place, the soul is bloodthirsty,
Words that come onto your tongue are traceries of a soul.
Hell with water and grass is better,
If there's no bazaar in every land.

The sons of beys have become cattle hands,
When a body will be able to withstand the poison of a serpent,
It'll come back injured to the city of Lut,
If every land is not governed by a brave man.

There are more ignorant men than wise ones in this world.
Ignorance is an evil, knowledge is life.
Those young men are no better than animals with a human's tongue,
If they don't have any dignity.

Poverty is a very bad evil for a young man,
He won't share his words with his friends,
Bad habit turns a friend into an alien,
Let it be driven out if it is not for the benefit of the nation.

God hasn't granted everyone a good beloved,
All his words are full with grief and he is full of sorrow,
Even if he lived up to a hundred years, he wouldn't enjoy even five days of life,
If a human being didn't have a companion he is worthy of.

Magtymguly, entrust yourself to Allah,
Don't lose your dignity in front of every coward,
I beg you forget this word of yours,
What the use of it if nobody is in need of it?

Temporary

Even the eyes capable of finding a black hair on a black stone,
Will worsen, because your eyesight is temporary.
Whoever comes to you, does not come for a treat, don't make your face sour,
He doesn't need your bread; he needs your cordial welcome.

Times are hard, roads are long,
When young men meet, and if they talk,
Colorful flowers will blossom in spring.
They will blossom just one season—they are temporary like guests of spring.

How great are jobs, how secret are deeds,
What fresh air in mountains, what tall trees,
Sixty colors and seventy kinds of fruit,
Will leave the trees, they are temporary; they are all guests of fall.

If a young man does not have a sword and a horse,
Keep this in mind, he has no zeal,
The older you become, the weaker become your bones,
The strength of a young man is temporary in his knees.

The Earth is a good place for you,
But it is full of sufferings and violence,
No matter how long you live, it will end with death,
Our sweet soul is temporary in our body.

If you remember the Lord and fear him,
Satan will come and won't leave you in peace,
Don't boast of your beauty, young youth;
You will become older—beauty is temporary, a guest on your face.

Magtymguly says, I always think of people,
I think of death with fear in my eyes,
No matter how long you will live in this cruel world,
The son of Adam is temporary, a guest for five days.

It Was There When the World Was Created

Though hundreds of thousands leave this world every day,
Still such an amount was there when the world was created,
If a hundred thousand abandon it due to their wrongdoings,
Still another hundred thousand lived a worthy life.

Hundreds of thousands of dervishes are in such a disastrous state,
Fasting all the time not having enough to eat,
In many a place one can see those who are crying,
There are also those who are happy and joyful.

If you travel throughout the four corners of the world,
You'll come across those who don't distinguish halal from haram, demons from devils;
Some would make their steady steps along the path they'd cleared,
Another hundred thousand are not caring about anything but their fixed routine.

It is such a chaotic time that it won't come to the people's minds,
Unfortunately nobody asked me, I would have told many useful things.
Where are Solomon, Rustem and the other courageous men?
Please don't tell me that still there are some, who found ways to stay.

Magtymguly don't fill your heart with sadness,
This is the time of work, so don't get lost in your thoughts,
Don't sit there speechless thinking that there is nobody to understand your words,
The world is vast, so there are some who know.

Will Not Come?

Oh fate, will the prosperous wheel of yours,
Come close and turn towards us?
Due to you so many bodies of brave men are put into graves,
Won't the Earth finally become conscious and be filled?

Oh, world, this bad habit of yours to take turns,
Turned the color of your teeth red because of blood,
So your acts remind us of a friendship between a goat and a wolf,
Won't there be time when a man in grief is happy, and the one who is crying is joyful?

You can mow down grass without a sickle, cut with no saber,
When slaughtering an animal you can skin it without your fist, hang it up without a rope,
You'll unexpectedly attack a weak man,
Won't he, who fights down a man, keep him underneath and not get off?

Fate will win regardless of whether you like it or fight it,
Straightening your body, stretching your wings,
Persuading a man to take death,
Won't he wither and turn yellow with fear?

Magtymguly, every morning, every dawn
Don't stay away from complaints and prayers,
If idols fulfill the wishes of the idolaters,
Won't he, who prays to the Almighty, get his wishes granted?

Will Turn into Black

If you use nut shells and juice of the red poppy
To dye your hair it will turn black.
Keep your soul away from bad, your tongue from gossip,
Otherwise the mirror of your soul will become dirty.

He who intends to commit evil,
Will endanger his deed in both worlds,
Whereas good manners and habits will turn your enemy into a good friend,
But your ill manners will do you only harm.

If a young man uses meaningless words,
He will be ashamed; his head will not be raised,
He who has not even a bit of faith,
Will have a heart like stone and black as night.

Such a human being is isolated from his people and full of sins,
Even a single word will be good for a good-natured man.
You will never know which one is a friend of Allah,
But much gratitude and blessings will bring you success.

Magtymguly, my word is short, but has much meaning.
It means nothing for a fool, but it has high value for the clever one.
One land is different from the other, as one man is not like the other.
But the problem is that when they talk they all sound equal.

Aiming

My seventy year old brother, don't try to shoot with a bow,
Its arrow won't hit the target no matter how much you aim.
Don't be proud of a building made of clay,
Clay won't stand long no matter how you try to fix it.

Humankind will have the sense of humanity,
An evil, insincere man will soon be disclosed by his rusty cover;
An evil man will bother faithful men,
He surely will argue over a piece of bread.

Do not choose an ill-natured one as a leader for your long journey,
Do not keep your soul far from Allah's order,
Do not share your sacred secrets with a fool,
Despite your efforts you won't keep water in a sieve.

Do not befriend an shrewd elderly man,
He will hide everything he has and show his empty pockets.
If the bowl of wisdom is emptied by the Almighty,
What's the use of decorating it outside?

Magtymguly, first of all, improve yourself,
People will think of this world, but you should share with them about Judgment Day.
Eat less, sleep less, and talk less,
What's the use of many meaningless words?

Gone in This Direction

Don't be proud of your wealth and riches,
Oh, what came from nowhere has gone in this direction.
Do not boast about deeds not worthy,
Many came and drowned in this mud.

These lands have seen many troubles,
How many hearts are burning due to these sufferings?
Many brave men abandoned them,
Whereas some have taken them for honey, and got themselves into a disaster.

Hey, clever young man, come here,
I've got some words; listen with all your heart.
Wherever you see a dervish, go, and get his blessings.
There is no one else better than a dervish for God!

A rich not paying his zakat deserves nothing but Hell,
Those who are disgraceful to dervishes are equal to stray dogs,
A dervish is a river on Earth, and the Moon in the sky,
What can a pig do to a river, a dog barking at the moon?

It is not a trustful land for a man to sleep.
Whoever is listening attentively, please, justify my words.
Magtymguly, make your advice so that they can keep it for the brave.
Who newly came to maintain the old palace?

Tears Are Flowing

The fog of grief is taking over my poor soul,
I cannot help crying, my tears are flowing.
Someone, taking mercy on me, asks about my state,
But seeing how depressed I am is giving me more pain.

Despite the efforts to increase the fire of love,
Death will be easier than a separation from a friend,
A separation threw me away from the mountain of patience,
A separation is taking my joints apart.

Initially my life went wrong due to Fate;
It has drained my bowl of sufferings and ignited a fire,
Love has burnt me down, it became too much,
And my heart is striving to free my body.

I was lying peacefully making plans,
My soul has been inspired with the desire to see my beloved,
Seeking God's assistance in fulfilling my wish,
My eyes are looking at those roads.

Magtymguly, I am still strong enough, let me have my say,
Let me make my grief evident to my friends.
Oh, friends, I have nothing to do but cry,
I am being burned down with love, I am on fire.

Far Behind

What joyful time is youth;
Spring has passed, it is far behind us now.
Old age has come accompanied with a thousand pains,
Fall equinox has passed, frost came, and winter has begun its reign.

I have spent my life always in a rush,
I did not find time for austerity or service to God,
I have spent my precious youth worthlessly,
Now I have neither strength nor inspiration.

Not a single bit of joy is left in my life,
No one will hear my bitter sufferings,
The fire of separation grilled my body,
Our hearts are bleeding; our eyes are full of tears.

Every servant suffers the pain of separation,
My body froze, its flowers withered.
The treasury is robbed, the house is burgled,
Neither mind, nor conscience is left.

Separation brought me a hundred thousand nights of grief,
My nights are endless, I can't wait for dawn's break.
It is a torture to spend a day in sadness,
Neither my soul is at peace, nor do I enjoy my life.

Separation caused lots of trouble to my soul and body,
I suffered a lot, now my body turned yellow,
My hair and beard turned gray because of my sufferings,
I have no joy in my soul, or pleasure in my heart.

Magtymguly, to quarrel is my only destiny,
My brain stopped thinking due to this evil separation,
I wonder what kind of deal this is, and what state I am in;
My soul got separated from my body and only flesh is left.

It Does Not Matter Whether It Is
a Hill or a Steppe

When riding a seven year old Arabian horse,
It does not matter whether you are on the hills or in the steppes.
For a mature brave young man,
It does not matter whether at fifty, sixty or a hundred.

A son of a coward will be scared of a field,
The trees he sees on either side will resemble men to him,
Cowards won't distinguish fog or dust
In the battlefield due to fear of the enemy.

Being a soldier not knowing a horse he is saddling,
Being a saint not knowing respect shown to him,
Not knowing the meaning of words during conversation,
Won't distinguish a gathering from a melody.

A crow will be lost in the fight of hunting birds and falcons,
It won't dare to appear near the battlefield,
In front of a hungry and furious falcon and its type,
Who won't distinguish ducks from geese.

Magtymguly, the words coming from your tongue inspire us,
Cowards were not given turn because of the power of your words,
Whether you are skilled or not in these crafts,
What is the word you are uttering with such power?!

Hesitation

Ignorance has put his head on its pillow,
A slumbering man spent so much time in hesitation.
The bird of life turned carnivorous in the cage of the body,
And is struggling to free itself with every breath.

Your life has passed; you haven't any good deeds,
You should have turned a stop on your path into a mosque, enjoying a hard mat of reeds.
Whatever you did is against your true belief, worth nothing,
Thus there is a bow with an arrow because you are indebted.

Take a piece of advice from good people,
Your caravan has left, hurry to catch up,
The son of Adam, be aware,
Insatiable Satan is waiting for you.

Eating at pleasure and getting dressed fancily,
Sleeping soundly and not thinking of fear,
The Lion of Death is ready for you, roaring and raising its paw.
Standing at your head, stretching from time to time.

Magtymguly, wake up, come to your senses,
Do not get into suffering, boasting about your wealth,
Don't put your life into the hands of the passing world,
The bottom of this blemish is quite obvious.

You Are So Inspired

Come my soul; look around at this world,
Tell me why you are so inspired.
Is there anyone else in this universe with a mouth like this world's?
Having revealed your secret, now you have been disclosed.

What would you do if they scold you, you hopeless man,
Saying: "Don't you have anyone in this world?"
Or due to strong love, not knowing your limits,
You have lost your senses.

If I go to the plains and deserts,
The soul will get excited, the tongue will abound with words,
People are amazed with you, whereas you are amazed by them.
Or have you lost your mind, as well as your consciousness?

Your speech and music are not everlasting,
There is no reliance on your winter or spring,
If you cannot free yourself from this grief on your own,
Why have you fallen into this furnace of sufferings?

Magtymguly, you've tried to go along various paths,
You have travelled a lot and spent time with many,
What have you seen in this world, what joys did you have?
By now when you have turned thirty-four?

The King, My Wanderer

Lovers are khans and sultans for everybody,
The king of the throne of the heavenly body, my wanderer,
I will cover distances searching for it,
I won't know which one; give me a message, my wanderer.

I suffered so much on this path,
Having gotten exhausted, I became miserable,
I brought with me Shibli, Mejnun,
Pyahlivan Piryar, Veyis, my wanderer.

I've inquired about her blossoming garden and flowers,
Their color faded due to severe wind,
She is very sad due to the unfaithful world,
Menewshe is mourning, my wanderer.

Neither am I in a mood to play or have fun,
The enemy won't let me come directly,
To meet and see my beloved in a secret place,
You have the sign of a friend, my wanderer.

My mind is full of thoughts days and nights,
I've spent all my time in this state.
Oh, Lord, if only you could share your bowl,
And just tell me the price for it, my wanderer.

If you show your love of the creator, Kadyr Suhan,
You will make me, the poor man, happy,
The mourning of a man in love has filled,
The entire world, the entire universe, my wanderer.

Magtymguly will say: the bones are yours,
The body is yours, the veins are yours, the blood is yours,
For its value the brain and soul are yours as well,
So, please, hold the bowl to my lips, my wanderer.

Shouldn't I Prepare?

There is no trust in life, nor continuation of the soul;
Shouldn't I prepare all I need for life in the Hereafter?
I am a slave with no other place to go,
Shouldn't I agree with the wish of the Almighty?

My dear friends, one cannot know the secrets of Suhan,
My only hope is to be blessed in my wish to acquire the best traits of a real friend,
Having put the load of hopelessness on the back of the camel of life,
Shouldn't I whip it up, guided by my zeal?

Burning in the torture of poverty, I dream about all that could be granted to me,
If I could water the tree of deficiency with my tears,
Shouldn't I give away my hypocrisy, arrogance,
And greed to the plunderers?

The boat of my dead body is being washed by the water of mercy,
If I can cross the cliff of divine service with honors,
By cherishing the bird of my spirit, the game of my soul,
Shouldn't I hunt from the forest of thoughts?

Magtymguly, what's the use of eating and drinking?
Your spirit will leave your body and your flesh will abandon your bones,
Your eyes will be unable to see, your tongue will be unable to speak,
Shouldn't I express my mind, while my tongue is still alive?

I Came Across

In the early morning hours while I was wandering,
I came across a nice place, a wonderful house,
Going one way or the other not knowing my direction,
I came across an amazing land and a beautiful palace.

I came across a bow set with no string,
Created by no master, tied with no string,
Sold with no price, kept with no hand,
Drawn with no touch, shot with no arrow.

Hoping that stars will guide me, I came across the Moon,
No matter how many friends he's been wandering with,
No matter, he found himself in the caravan, having lost the row,
No matter how surprised he was, having lost his hope for life.

With all my heart I liked the sherbet my friends drank,
They are having hundreds of joys, but I am suffering thousands of grievances,
Having been separated, I am moaning, but I retain my strength,
I have been looking for a spring to drink water from, but I came across a gully.

I have neither power in my body, nor a soul within,
I don't know whether there is benefit or harm in this,
There is neither count, nor a known quantity,
I came across an affair no one knows about.

Putting a rope of madness over my head,
On a fast horse I was by my beloved in no time,
I reached out my hand to the red wine and stared,
The pure wine was gone, I came across mud instead.

Magtymguly is my name,
The entire world can warm their hands over my fire,
Oh, my friends, who can I tell about my sufferings,
I came across an affair I do not know about.

Oh, You, World

The day will come when ships well-travelled,
will be turned over with your order, oh, crazy world.
If no one ever comes to see you,
You will mislead him saying that the wealth is here, oh, this world.

You might be aware that whenever your breath stops,
The step you take forward will turn into a grave,
You will lay a road across a man, oh, world,
Who is unaware of the life around.

There is no peace or patience, no end to it for you,
You won't kill your thirst even if you drink blood day and night,
First you will give us honey to gain our trust,
One day you will poison our food, oh, you, world.

You will come with no notice and threaten me,
You will spend your time by doing good and evil,
One day will mix the poison with our meal,
Deceivingly you give honey first, the crazy world.

Seasons go round, winter, spring, summer and fall,
Mountains, seas and plains, all, appear good in every season,
We also go through these changes too in the end,
You will be left all by yourself in the state you are, oh, you, world.

You killed many; more were swallowed,
You have swallowed the soul of Allah's prophet Mohammad,
You have swallowed Croesus and Aaron, Solomon,
This is what you do, this is certain, oh, you, world.

You have caused endless pains to the son of Adam,
All, young and old, wander on your way,
You are like a female donkey in the state of heat,
Your bosom is full of grief, oh, you, world.

Magtymguly, you won't be aware of the secrets of this world,
The people whom we see today, you won't leave until tomorrow,
You keep on eating for so long, but do not satiate,
Oh, you, falling, collapsing and barefaced world.

Caught with Fire

My dear friends, due to the challenges of this cruel world,
My heart is caught with fire.
My body is aching like the body of Eyyup,
No one will know, this wound is speechless.

Days and nights all I do is moan;
I'm all in tears wandering around.
Whenever on the lake I will cry:
I am drowned, oh, courageous pirs, I am in need of your help.

He who is poor will wander in poor places,
Shedding tears filled with blood.
He who loves will meet his beloved,
The flowers will blossom, and he will get inspired upon seeing her.

Sow your seeds, you'll bring the harvest in;
Coming to this world do not spend your life in vain.
You will have a look around this world,
It is an old, old world, once visited; people come and leave, not staying long.

Magtymguly, his soul is caught with fire,
His heart is overfilled with blood; his eyes are full of tears;
He became so miserable, pleading for help everywhere,
But no one is taking pity; I have such a bad fate.

Grief Will Not Remain

A garden that once was full of nightingales,
A nightingale itself will leave you, and grief will not remain.
Rainy, snowy and foggy mountains,
Mudflows will leave you, the fog will not remain.

Sons of Adam were created different from each other,
Some tall, some short; some wise, others fools; some with a conscience and some without,
The time of youth resembles the season of spring,
But the spring will leave you, it will not remain.

Welcome anyone who comes with honor, if you can.
Keep your intentions in compliance with good will,
Let generosity be your companion in life,
This life will pass, it will not remain.

This world is turbulent, full of conflicts.
Some are busy with charity; others are busy with greed.
Young men, this world is like this, indeed,
By pouring out its glittering drops from the skies, the rain will not remain.

It is a temporary stop where you enjoy food and drink for three days,
But after four days when you've just settled,
Feeling at ease and relaxed, they will stir you up,
A guest will not remain for more than five days.

A day will come when the soil will embrace and hide you,
These fragile eyes will be filled with black soil,
Do not boast, the meadows are full of flowers;
The flowers will leave you, festivities will not remain.

Magtymguly will say to his wise friend,
Who can flee from the hands of the angel of death?
A day will come when you will be placed in the soil,
The tongue will leave your mouth, your speech will not remain.

You Will Be Disclosed

Do not confide your secrets in those lacking courage;
They will reveal your secrets, you will be disclosed.
Do not become the neighbor of a robber and a swindler in the village,
They will deprive you of your wealth, thus turn you into a needy man.

Do not befriend the fools,
Never on Earth have a word with cowards.
Do not turn away from your trusted friend,
Whenever you visit him, he will consider you a crown on his head.

If a brave young man falls in love with a good-natured beauty,
And if he desires to see her at least once,
If there is an evil man in between,
He will ruin your good relations with your best friend.

Sufis won't make mistakes when reading prayers,
All your sins will be forgiven if you get up at dawn,
Never on Earth make rumors or get involved in lewdness,
Otherwise you will encounter the fire of Hell.

Magtymguly, you spread your advice amongst the people,
Never on Earth make friends with the evil-natured,
If God grants you a propitious child,
He will make you younger when you grow old.

Imagine

If you are caught in a corner before you had a chance to see the world,
Imagine that you were set up to travel the world on a horse as fast as the wind.
Imagine that you have skills in many crafts, both old and new,
In countries such as China, India, the Roman Empire and Ethiopia.

Never engage yourself in begging even if you are hungry,
Say to yourself: "I am in a palace; my head has reached the sky."
If you happen to be in the desert and cannot find any shade,
Imagine you found shade in the Garden of Eden.

Whenever you are offered food, do not hasten,
Even if you are too hungry, do not reveal that to the people around.
Having won the support of real servants by spreading gold and silver,
Even if you die young, imagine that you've reached the age of Noah.

If no one, except God, knows that you are in need,
The living is enough if one does not die of hunger.
If you do not own clothes like Indians do,
Imagine that you possess a whole bundle of the Shah's clothes.

Such people like Suleyman, whose orders were followed,
By the water and wind, are no longer in this world.
If you are in a desert and you are dying from thirst,
Imagine yourself as if you are Iskender in the river.

Imagine if you become a companion to an ant, which does not understand you,
If you cannot find a place to sleep other than with the snake,
Imagine that you have seized the treasury of Karun,
Twenty six times with the help of a hundred thousand brave men.

Magtymguly, even though you are suffering and in pain,
Know that being thankful and patient will please God,
Know that your live body is like a grave for your soul, thin as hair,
And though your tongue is alive, imagine that you are dead.

With the Wind

My eyes, my soul, tongue and mind—all four stayed behind,
My soul rose with the wind yearning for my motherland,
Please, I beg you; do not abandon this land,
Enjoy your life, speak to the flowers.

It's a wonderful place; do not lose your hope,
Do not lose your passion; do not get angry with your country,
Do not ruin your shops, devastate your bazaars,
Stay with the wealth of your body for several days.

You have been a guest at the house of this world,
Do not follow its intentions by being attracted,
It will keep you busy with its thoughts, capturing your mind,
If you do adhere, it will deceive you and always hold you tight.

If you are a servant here, you will be granted the entire world there,
All delicacies of various kinds and freshly prepared food will be yours,
Paradise, the Byrag horse, the fairies of Paradise will be yours,
If you, you poor man, will take the right path.

Fate will leave no one on the land where life once was enjoyed,
A wolf and a sheep don't get along in the same place,
What's the use of enormous riches you've collected?
Whatever you have given with your own hand will be your only wealth, indeed.

Even if the sky is brought down and spread onto the land,
A wolf won't be able to catch a lamb.
The courageous fighters won't be able to support themselves,
An elephant, tied with a single hair, will stand, not being able to move.

Magtymguly, if you fulfill the Divine service,
He, who will comply with the Divine order, will be a real man.
If God himself is present for the council,
Then even a mosquito will be able to argue with an elephant.

The Failed Fate

Many young men came and left this world,
Their fate has failed their dreams.
Everything goes wrong due to unlucky fate,
He, who was happy in the morning, isn't laughing anymore.

The angel of death will tailor grave-clothes every day,
It is such a misfortune; this hunt will never end,
It will bring down an endless number of people,
Those, whom we saw today, didn't stay until tomorrow.

Take my advice, listen to my words,
The world's face is like a changing home.
When the angel of death comes, a person's eyes close,
We'll never know whether he came to this world or not.

Where is Feridun, who split the world into four,
Harun who built the wealthy palace of Humayun,
And Karun who filled forty cities with gold,
Whose eyes had been filled with sand, but never satiated with gold.

Magtymguly is amazed, he is looking around,
Oh what a miracle, fire is coming out of water,
A good son will become a source of endless blessings,
A son who brings disgrace would be better if he were unborn.

A Stranger is Better

A stranger is better to have around on your
Day of happiness, visiting each other.
But your close friend, your brother, as well as your wealth
Are good on your sad days, when you are in trouble.

Get yourself involved in halal deeds – you will be blessed in the hereafter.
Don't hurt the poor – your soul is merciful,
A man in love will say you have enough wisdom,
If you are wise, listen to my words attentively.

A son, someone's progeny, is the support for his heart,
His sweet love will provide strength to your bones,
Every young man aims to achieve these three goals:
He needs love, he needs a weapon, and a horse will be good too.

The mullahs will read the last prayer for the dead,
Don't be doubtful, they do the right thing,
Who knows what they are going to do in the hereafter?
So, enjoy your life to the full, eating and drinking before you die.

If God grants high spirits to a human's soul,
The food will go into his mouth even if someone tries to stop his hand,
If wealth takes its path, it will find its way,
A stranger is better when he intends to come or go.

He who doesn't adhere to a man's advice or word,
Is not better than a dry willow,
A caring dog in your stable is better
Than a young man who doesn't respect his friends, or understand anything.

Magtymguly, don't hide your secrets from a friend,
Do not search for an unfaithful stranger,
Keep silence; do not talk in the gathering,
If you decide to talk, first think your words over very well.

A Guest to the Waist

A son of Adam, do not be content with your life,
Your youth is a guest to your knees and waist.
Also do not be lazy when serving God,
The steps you take are a guest to the road.

The soil that will embrace you is your place of birth;
You are a caravan, you will move to your permanent abode.
The flowers of the season will wither; you will fade and pass away.
Your voice will stop; it is a guest of your tongue.

Some will be engaged in the Divine service,
Others will be engaged in music,
Some will favor gambling, and others hunting.
Drakes that once enjoyed their time are guests of the lake.

Look friends, there is no lie in these words of mine,
I am a poor man, whose advice is not heeded,
Magtymguly, no one is aware of my grief,
The remedy for my pain is a guest of the tongue.

Beys

The act of the brave man won't match one of a coward,
Oh, beys, cowards will only do harm in battle.
A coward won't know the value of a brave man,
Oh, beys, each deed of a coward is a disaster.

Mature brave men won't cheat to take your share,
Whereas cowards will never be satisfied even with the wealth of the entire world.
A coward won't adhere to advice or suggestions,
Oh, beys, each deed of a coward is obvious, indeed.

Each father has his features taken from his six forefathers,
A coward has thoughts of a hundred intentions in his head.
Brave men will be offered a house wherever they go,
Oh, beys, a coward's own house is like a prison for him.

When he finds wealth, he forgets his friends,
When a disaster comes, he will be tied to his bed with grief,
Still he will not start believing that everything comes from God.
Magtymguly, this is reality nowadays, oh beys.

My Fate, My Cruel Enemy

You separated me, my fate, my cruel enemy,
From my parents, brothers and a son.
You've distanced me from my people, my will and my wealth,
You separated me, my fate, my cruel enemy.

Stretching out hands, I cannot hit the target due to my poverty,
The sorrow of my heart will never get healed, won't go away.
It will not decrease no matter how much I plead to God,
You separated me, my fate, my cruel enemy.

I am indebted, I am living through the days of suffering.
I don't know what disaster there is for me,
I have got neither wisdom nor thoughts in my head,
You separated me, my fate, my cruel enemy.

What harm did I do to your craft?
Come and sit down here, my wretched fate,
Get Pyragy out of your head from now on
You separated me, my fate, my cruel enemy.

Catching

Fate has spread its net throughout this world,
Catching all living creatures no matter what.
It captured many poor, set up an army,
It is driving them all through the mountains and plains.

No one can run away, it will catch you no matter what,
It will attack you, strike you, and hold you by your collar,
It will throw your body into an underground dungeon,
It will mix your body with the black soil.

What a time it is, what intentions fate has,
It will find its way to the city of the soul,
The destiny of the son of Adam is such that he gets mixed into mud,
It then will be beat down with a hammer.

Magtymguly, struggling with his eyes blind-folded,
He suffered, rolling in the grave,
Travelling in all directions of this transient world,
Fate is swallowing all of the people.

In Need of a Ruler

Nations with dignity and power,
Are in need of a brave and rich ruler.
Waists have no value with only a belt,
For that a beautiful red robe is also needed.

A precious dream and your beautiful face,
The haze of mountains, the wind of the Hazar Sea,
A rich man with a sense of dignity and wealth,
Is in need of a sharp saber and a fast horse.

Magtymguly, don't dwell on this grief,
This era is full of sufferings, but no joy,
Both of the worlds are related to man,
He is in need of honor and faith, the pupil of his eyes.

My Beautiful Beloved Won't Be Seen

Wake up, let me ask Gabriel,
What is the reason for my beautiful beloved not to be seen?
I am ready to come to your doors every day, begging you to let me in,
I promise – yet my zeal will not be noticed.

Fate has made its grindstones impatient,
Being distanced from its dignity, it was shamed by God,
Young men grew older, the elderly became young,
My candle was extinguished, my fire can't be seen.

Envious men became brave, poor became kings,
Brave men became cowards, pirs forgot their religion,
Calls to prayer stopped, mosques closed,
Not a single deed will be hidden from the sight of God.

Magtymguly says, what kind of phenomenon is this,
All people are now "scholars," and won't listen to advice,
Disaster descended from the sky to the earth,
Jesus, Mati, Malik the Dragon won't be seen.

Won't Know His Path

If an Indian separates from his companion elephant,
He won't know that time passed and the destination arrived,
If Karun is apart from his evil intentions,
He won't be satiated, won't perceive the world's treasure.

If a lame man is apart from his cane,
An old man without his companion won't see his way,
If a brave burning man bites a mountain,
He won't know a black stone, fog or mudflows.

The signs of Death won't come to an end beforehand,
The head will not distinguish either feet or hands when it comes across them,
The son of Adam will burn and suffer,
Neither Satan nor the saint will know his intentions.

The hopeless is enamored when his beloved is far away,
When the heart is burning and tears are running from blind eyes,
If Jemshid meets a suffering brave man,
He won't know Alexander the Great, or Rustem, the son of Zal.

If fortune fails, both eyes will become blind,
The paths of those, who went in search of charity, will be blocked,
A single sin will fester in the soul of a brave man,
He will start cutting with his sword, unaware of his left or right.

Magtymguly, a destan came onto my tongue,
I spent my days and months in sadness and in grief,
I brought my pleas to the top,
He will pass by, not perceiving the months and years.

My Soul

Oh my soul, that died before the Angel of Death came, wake up from the darkness!
Having lost hope in this world, plead to the Creator, oh my soul.
Only a brave one can please this poor soul of mine,
My soul that smiled at whomever it saw has fallen into the bottomless river,
The soul is transient; this world is transient, wrap yourself with grave clothes, my soul,
Fill it with words until it is full of them, my soul.

Listen to the words of scientists, get their advice,
Get up and raise your hands in prayer to your Lord,
Pick up and carry the challenges of this transient world tying them on to your back,
Only brave ones can do this, so be brave, stand up and carry,
Be worthy of a mature person, stay away from liars,
Go to the burial of an honored pir, and repent by falling onto his dust, my soul.

I have such a love that is sixty times stronger than that of Mejnun,
I have enough strength to teach Perhat for forty years,
If only I succeed to go and see my Lord with a fire in my heart.
Oh, how I wish to have my dream fulfilled with the overflowing of our Lord's river of bounty.
If you lose your soul in this world, you will not be able to get it back once lost,
Only a brave one can please this poor soul of mine.

Read your prayer at dawn to get the blessing of the angel,
What's the use of slumbering, and forgetting your Lord.
Even thousands of riches won't give you access to the entire wealth of the world,
Put on the gown of a dervish, go get mixed up with crazy men,
Otherwise you will remain lonely, lost and sad,
Let your deeds match your words, oh, my soul.

Magtymguly, two glasses were enough to kill my sadness,
Yet, there was no desire to drink the third; I got rid of my true soul,
There are numerous contradictory thoughts in my head, and Satan is constantly inside me.
Let's find a solution to this suffering, oh my people,
Even if Isa, Hydyr, and Ilyas kneel and try to heal,
My soul, that is almost dead, won't recover and live again.

My Arabic-Speaking Beloved

They stained your dress in blood,
My famous beloved speaking Arabic,
In separation, the soul of your father burnt down,
My famous Arabic-speaking beloved,
My sweetheart, originally from Syria, dressed in a Roman outfit.

Shedding endless tears due to sufferings,
Being afraid of the wolves in the steppes,
You've left your father and the land of Kengan,
My famous Arabic-speaking beloved,
My sweetheart, originally from Syria, dressed in a Roman outfit.

Being dressed lightly your tender skin got damaged,
The mountain of separation was put against your chest,
The eyes of Jacob went blind from crying so much.
My famous Arabic-speaking beloved,
My sweetheart, originally from Syria, dressed in a Roman outfit.

Your brothers have arrived immediately, crying bitterly.
Having got scared even the wolves came running.
All who came stood astonished at the edge of the pit.
My famous Arabic-speaking beloved,
My sweetheart, originally from Syria, dressed in a Roman outfit.

Magtymguly, the entire world has been looked through,
Destiny brought you to Egypt and abandoned you,
Then being regretful, prostrated himself before you,
My famous Arabic-speaking beloved,
My sweetheart, originally from Syria, dressed in a Roman outfit.

Dedicate, Pyragy

Having taken the world's beauty in your hands
Do grant it to your people, before you pass away.
Don't conceal all things, whether good or bad.
Dedicate them to your nation, Pyragy.

Let other nations who lack it look at it from aside, striving for it.
Let the river Jeyhun full of waters flow to Gurgen.
Let your beautiful nation abandon the state of unawareness.
Dedicate it to your nation before you pass away, Pyragy.

What can be done about it, many cowards have failures?
They demonstrated their good nature to humanity and were appreciated.
Saintly men getting together expressed their blessings,
Dedicate it to your nation before you pass away, Pyragy.

Don't be hopeful for the wealth of envious men,
Follow the path of courageous men,
Don't give a bayonet into the hands of a coward, he won't keep it.
Dedicate it to your nation before you pass away, Pyragy.

Don't regret shedding tears from your eyes,
Don't leave, having totally abandoned your Motherland,
Sacrifice your soul by drinking wine
And having fun; instead,

Say everything, if your words praise God.
Take mercy on your nation; don't make a secret of it.
Let the words you utter be always precious like diamonds,
Dedicate it to your nation before you pass away, Pyragy.

Make yourself happy day and night,
Let Turks, Bulgarians, and Persians be amazed,
By cypress-like gracious, gentle, sweet-smelling beauty,
Dedicate it to your nation before you pass away, Pyragy.

Don't lose your dignity having confronted disaster,
Gather your people around yourself,
Paradise will appear in front of you, wishing to see you.
Dedicate it to your nation before you pass away, Pyragy.

Let your tongue utter frank words, you are highly respected;
Your head will be free from pain; you'll assemble a big gathering by reading "Zuha"
You are welcome; in front of you "zuýýenes-sema"
To the land of Ferewan, to the water of Kowsar,

With your greetings give your nation a destan sweet as honey,
Dedicate it to your nation before you pass away, Pyragy.
Don't forget the poor,
thinking of yourself as a man of wisdom,

Don't join cowards,
thinking you're more informed than they are,
Wishing to be free, don't betray your fascinating destan,
Dedicate it to your nation before you pass away, Pyragy.

If the nation is invaded by the enemy, hesitate not to suppress it,
Be brave enough like Gorogly, gather all your might to attack it,
Don't try to add more effort other than this in this deed,
Dedicate it to your nation before you pass away, Pyragy.

Make your nation glorious to the world,
Always bring more and more benefit by your hands,
You've done many deeds to be proud of,
Dedicate them to your nation before you pass away, Pyragy.

The plant of the Garden of Eden has turned your land into an orchard,
Her face like a full moon reminds me of the Paradise,
Black curls of her hair are "Welleyli"; her eyebrows are like a crescent in the dark sky,
Dedicate it to your nation before you pass away, Pyragy.

Magtymguly, you are an aged man now,
You've always been a companion to good-natured people,
You've got the blessings of skillful brave men,
Dedicate it to your nation before you pass away, Pyragy.

Endnotes

1 Jeyhun is an archaic name of the Amu Darya, a river that runs along the eastern border of Turkmenistan.

2 Hazar is an archaic name of the Caspian Sea, still often used in Turkmen. The Caspian Sea is at the western border of Turkmenistan.

3 One of the Turkmen tribes.

4 A wild donkey

5 Type of literary work which includes both poetry and prose.

6 Magtymguly's sister, who died when he was 21.

7 According to oral tradition, Magtymguly's sister Hanmengli, brother Janesen, and his wife Bayram, all died on the same day and the poet composed this poem at that time, at the age of twenty-one.

8 Pyrak means "separation" in Persian, thus "pyragy" refers to a person who is separated from someone.

9 The Prophet Mohammad

Poem Titles in English and Turkmen

For those wishing to examine these translations against the original Turkmen poem, this table provides our English titles alongside the Turkmen titles as used in Ashirov's 2-volume compilation of selected poems by Magtymguly (*Magtymguly: Eserler ýygyndysy*, compiled by A. Ashirov [Turkmen: A. Aşyrow]; edited by R. Godarov [Turkmen: R. Godarow]. Ashgabat: Institute of Manuscripts, Turkmenistan Academy of Sciences [Türkmenistanyň Ylymlar akademiýasynyň, Milli golýazmalar instituty], 2013.) Ashirov's listing and index of Turkmen poem titles can be found in his volume 2, pp. 531-543. As noted in the Preface, all titles of these poems were added by later commentators, not by Magtymguly.

Page numbers at right indicate the first page of the poem in the present volume.